Trading with the Trendlines
Harmonic Pattern Strategy

DAVID CARLI

Trading foreign exchange on margin carries a high level of risk, and may not be suitable for all investors. The high degree of leverage can work against you as well as for you. Before deciding to invest in foreign exchange, you should carefully consider your investment objectives, level of experience, and risk appetite. No information or opinion contained in this book should be taken as a solicitation or offer to buy or sell any currency, or other financial instruments or services. Past performance is no indication or guarantee of future performance.

Copyright © Fifth edition April 2020 by David Carli.

All rights reserved. This book or any portion thereof may not be reproduced or used in any manner whatsoever without the express written permission of the publisher except for the use of brief quotations in a book review.

The book images 1 to 9 were created by me, I have the PSD files and are copyrighted. Images 10 to 51 are charts taken from TradingView.com. As stated in point 4 of their Privacy (https://www.tradingview.com/policies/) I am authorised to use these charts. So, for Amazon and others, this book does not break any laws.

First Printing: 2016

ISBN: 9798645896652

Website: www.tradingwithdavid.com
E-mail: info@tradingwithdavid.com

EDITED

Caroline Winter
carolinewinter4@hotmail.com

CONTENTS

Introduction – About the Author   1

Introduction – About TradingView   2

Introduction – Preface   3

Chapter 1 – Harmonic Patterns   4

Chapter 2 – The Strategy   14

Chapter 3 – Pullback   40

Chapter 4 – Money Managements   52

Chapter 5 – Final Comments   55

Appendix A – Strategy Parameters   58

Appendix B – Web Resources   61

ABOUT THE AUTHOR
INTRODUCTION

My journey in the investment and trading world started shortly after I graduated from the University of Pisa, Italy. I then travelled to New York City USA., where I attended exclusive courses by Steve Nison who introduced the western world to the art of the Japanese candlestick as a tool for analysing market trends and investment decisions.

I have been working as a full-time trader and an independent financial analyst since 2007 hence I established Trading with David as a niche investment service with the primary focus on FX markets and commodities. During that time, I collaborated with reputable financial trading services and investment magazines. And from 2012 -2013 I worked as a hedge fund manager for an Italian Bank boutique. In 2018, I began providing market analysis and trading ideas for a major European commodity investment company up to this date.

I published several trading and investment books to pass on my knowledge and expertise on how to analyse the financial market correctly and have the odds on your side to become a profitable trader. My approach is based on low-risk investment strategies across all markets to achieve a balanced asset allocation through diversification and risk management.

I have several other books for those who wish to learn more about certain aspects of trading such as Forex, Commodities Spread Trading, and Options so you can see how I approach other markets. Through educational channels, I coach independent investors on my personal trading strategies and how to apply them in different market conditions.

You can find out more about my educational library on https://tradingwithdavid.com to develop an extraordinary edge to your trading and investments plan with a deep understanding of the macro environment, along with advanced analysis and risk management they are designed to build or improve your trading skills.

ABOUT TRADINGVIEW
INTRODUCTION

My favourite trading platform is TradingView. While I have used many other platforms in the past, I have found this innovative platform has all tools and versatility that once were only reserved for investment firms' players. The popularity of this platform among active traders ranging from institutional traders, financial software companies, and retail traders is a testament to its user-friendly interface.

Created by MultiCharts as a browsing web-based charting platform. It offers a multitude of features that allow market enthusiasts to connect and collaborate via a chat window, sharing ideas and exchange opinions in real-time - this is particularly useful for those who wish to follow a certain style of trading by following specific members without the need to subscribe to their chat room at an extra cost.

Another feature that is extremely important for active traders is the ease of writing scripts. The programming language that TradingView designed is called Pine Script, it's lightweight yet powerful which lets anyone develop their own proprietary indicators and strategies to be published on the community hub.

The platform has one of the largest social networks driven by traders and investors who contribute trading ideas for the public to interact with and learn from – a place where top analysis and valuable content are presented daily by professional traders globally. With over 100 ready-to-use indicators, and over 5000 scripts commonly used for researching and backtesting. TradingView lets you discover a new world of trading and showcase your talent by being a part of a dynamic and robust community of traders.

And if speed of trade execution is your priority, TradingView allows you to integrate your account directly with your brokerage account.

Personalization is truly the greatest aspect of this platform; you could build spreads and compare two or more charts with ease. Every single instrument can be customised, and every detail can be modified. It has been my preferred charting platform for all the reasons mentioned above and more - you will be able to follow my new trading ideas and the articles that I regularly publish on TradingView to expand your knowledge and improve your trading.

PREFACE
INTRODUCTION

"Harmonic Patterns Strategy" is the first volume of the series "Trading with the Trendlines." The book explains a strategy applicable in every market (forex, equities, commodity...), based on a harmonic pattern and trendline.

You will see harmonic patterns from a different perspective. The strategy, in fact, is not used in a classical way, but seeks to exploit the completion of a Gartley or Butterfly, trying to ride the last leg.

Therefore, what you are going to read in this book is my personal interpretation of this type of pattern. A way to predict a future movement of a market, which I have elaborated after observing many similar situations, and identifying a subsequent trend common to many cases that share certain conditions.

Identifying the target profit and stop-loss of this strategy is both easy and clear. Not only this, but depending on your account, I will also explain the correct position sizing so that you can properly manage your money. If you are a beginner, do not worry; the first two chapters will provide you with adequate knowledge for understanding the strategy and using it correctly.

Do not be tricked by the fact that this book is widely distributed at printing price. The strategy, if you use it correctly and with the appropriate money management for your account, will give you a high percentage of profitable trades. However, combining this strategy with fundamental analysis is recommended, as is opening a position only if both give the same signal.

For any question, do not hesitate to contact me at the e-mail address info@tradingwithdavid.com, it will be my pleasure to answer all of you. Also, visit my website https://tradingwithdavid.com, where you will find free articles, analyses, and books.

Harmonic Patterns

CHAPTER 1

What is Harmonic Trading? As defined by Scott M. Carney, Harmonic Trading is a methodology that utilises the recognition of specific price patterns and the alignment of exact Fibonacci ratios to determine highly probable reversal points in the financial markets.

This methodology assumes that trading patterns or cycles, like many patterns and cycles in life, repeat themselves. The key is to identify these patterns and to enter or exit a position based upon a high degree of probability that the same historic price action will occur.

Harmonic Trading utilises the best strategies of Fibonacci and pattern recognition techniques to identify, execute, and manage trade opportunities. These techniques are extremely precise and comprise a system that requires specific conditions to be met before any trade is executed.

Its approach offers information regarding the potential state of future price action like no other technical methods. The unique measurements and price point alignment requirements are some of the unprecedented methods that differentiate this approach from other technical perspectives.

Harmonic Trading techniques are similar to standard technical price patterns, such as the Head and Shoulders or Wedge formations, since the focus on a particular shape of price action is the key validation factor. However, harmonic patterns are probably the most specific technical price patterns due to the specific Fibonacci measurements of each point within the structure.

These measurements provide a tremendous advantage in that they serve to quantify and categorise similar price structures as distinct "technical entities." Depending upon the specific alignment of Fibonacci ratios within each structure, potential trading opportunities can be differentiated, offering pattern-specific strategies for each situation.

In essence, similar price structures are not the same, and each pattern has to be precisely defined. From such specification, a great deal of information can be garnered regarding the state of potential price action.

What is a Harmonic pattern? Harmonic patterns were born in the thirties, thanks to H. M. Gartley. He noticed the frequency with which precise patterns formed in price movements.

Harmonic patterns are defined by specific price structures quantified by Fibonacci calculations. Essentially, these patterns are price structures that contain combinations of distinct and consecutive Fibonacci retracements and projections.

The primary theory behind harmonic patterns is price/time movements which adhere to Fibonacci ratio relationships and its symmetry in markets. Fibonacci ratio analysis works well with any market and on any timeframe chart.

The basic idea of using these ratios is that, by calculating the various Fibonacci aspects of a specific price structure, you identify a specific area to examine for potential turning points in price action, retracements, and projections along with a series of swing high and swing low points. The derived projections and retracements using these swing points (highs and lows) give key price levels for targets or stops.

Let's proceed in order. I talked about Fibonacci retracements and projections. In Appendix C, you will find a brief biography of Fibonacci, As well as number sequences, ratios, etc. Now I want to define what Fibonacci retracements, extensions, projections and expansions are.

- **Retracement**: from the swing XA, a Fibonacci ratios length is retraced to B, as shown in figure 1.

Figure 1 - Fibonacci retracement

- **Extension**: from the swing XA, more than 100% of the swing XA is extended from A to B, as you can see in figure 2.

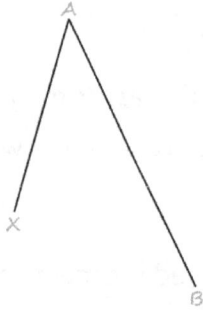

Figure 2 - Fibonacci extension

- **Projection**: from the swing XA, a retracement is made to form the AB leg. From B, the swing XA is projected from B to C (figure 3).

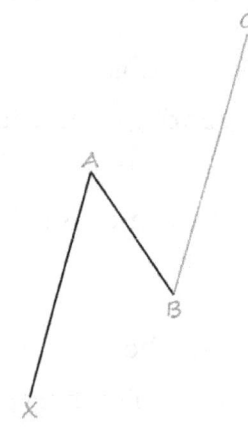

Figure 3 - Fibonacci projection

- **Expansion**: from the swing XA, a retracement is made to form the AB leg. An expansion is an impulse wave in the direction of the trend from A to C with the same length of XA, as shown in figure 4.

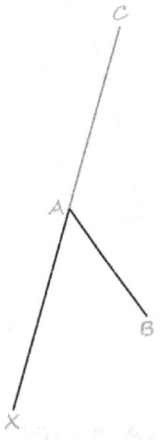

Figure 4 - Fibonacci expansion

You can see everything explained above in a picture (figure 5).

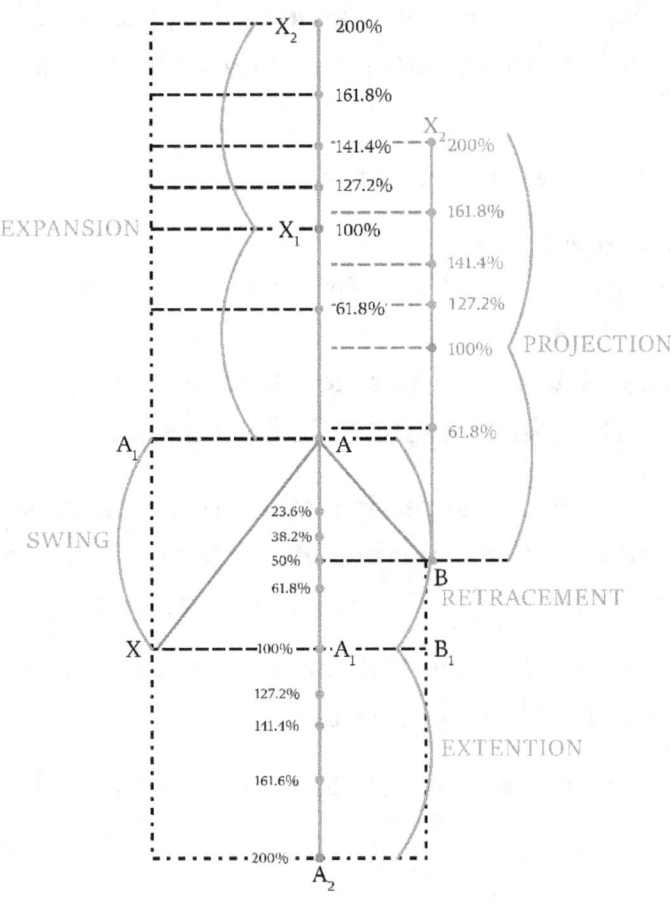

Figure 5 - Types of Fibonacci levels

Harmonic Trading utilises an enormous array of effective Fibonacci alignment combinations to define patterns. I am not arrogant enough to try and explain such a vast and complex argument in a handful of pages; what I will illustrate below are only the Harmonic Patterns "involved" in my strategy.

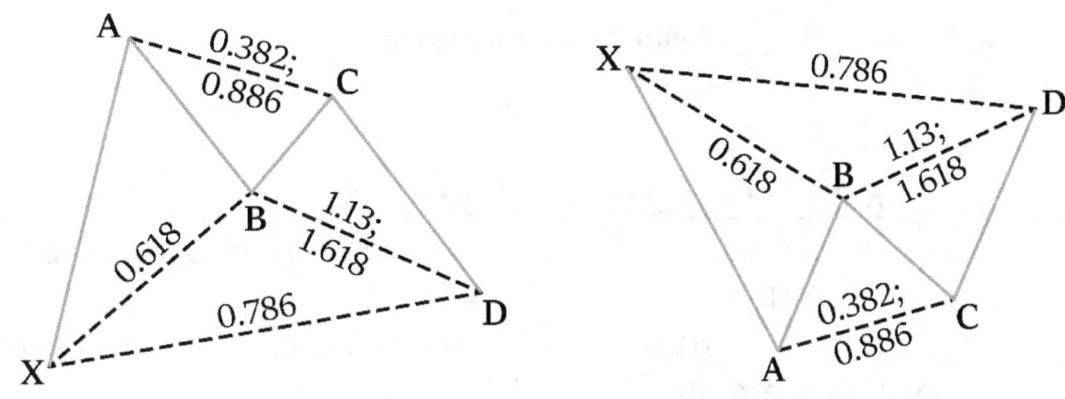

Figure 6 - The Gartley pattern

- The <u>Gartley</u> pattern (also known as Gartley 222) is the most famous Harmonic Pattern. It is named after its creator, Harold Gartley, who published it for the first time in his book "Profit in the Stock Market." In figure 6 above, the Gartley pattern, alongside the Fibonacci calculations.

In 1999, Scott Carney redefined the structure as follows:

- ✓ <u>B = 0.618 of XA</u>;
- ✓ C = from 0.382 to 0.886 (it means: 0.382, 0.500, 0.618, 0.707, 0.786, or 0.886) of AB;
- ✓ D = from 1.13 to 1.618 (it means: 1.130, 1.272, 1.414, or 1.618) of BC;
- ✓ <u>D = 0.786 of XA (sometimes 0.886 of XA)</u>.

Of course, these iron rules greatly facilitate the identification of this pattern but at the same time reduce the chances that it is complete perfectly. So, you will not frequently find a pattern that respects all these conditions. The rules I have underlined are fundamental.

- Scott Carney created the <u>Bat</u> pattern in 2001. It is characterised by deep retracements that often retest supports or resistances.

In figure 7 is the Bat pattern, alongside all the Fibonacci calculations.

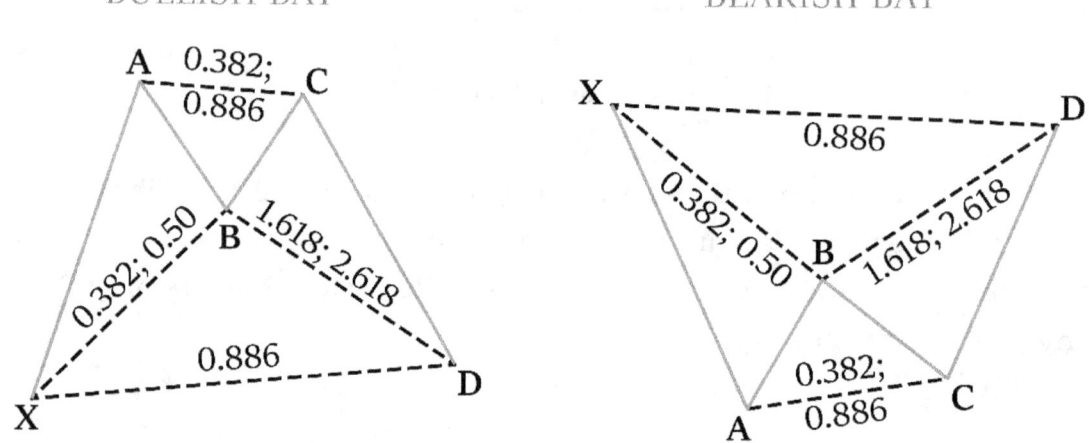

Figure 7 - The Bat pattern

The pattern structure:

- ✓ B = <u>0.382 or 0.500</u> of XA (ideal 0.500);
- ✓ C = from 0.382 to 0.886 (it means: 0.382, 0.500, 0.618, 0.707, 0.786, or 0.886) of AB;
- ✓ D = from 1,618 to 2,618 (it means: 1.618, 2.000, 2.240, or 2.618) of BC (1.618 or 2.000 the ideal);
- ✓ <u>D = 0.886 of XA</u>.

Point B is the element that distinguishes a Bat from a Gartley pattern. If the retracement to point B stops no more than 50% of the XA movement, then it is considered a Bat pattern; otherwise, it is a Gartley pattern. CD cannot be less than 1.618 BC; otherwise, the pattern is invalidated.

• Bryce Gilmore created the **Butterfly** pattern and later, Scott Carney went on to define with more precision the relationship between the various "legs," all to facilitate a more successful trading.

In figure 8 the Butterfly, alongside all the Fibonacci calculations.

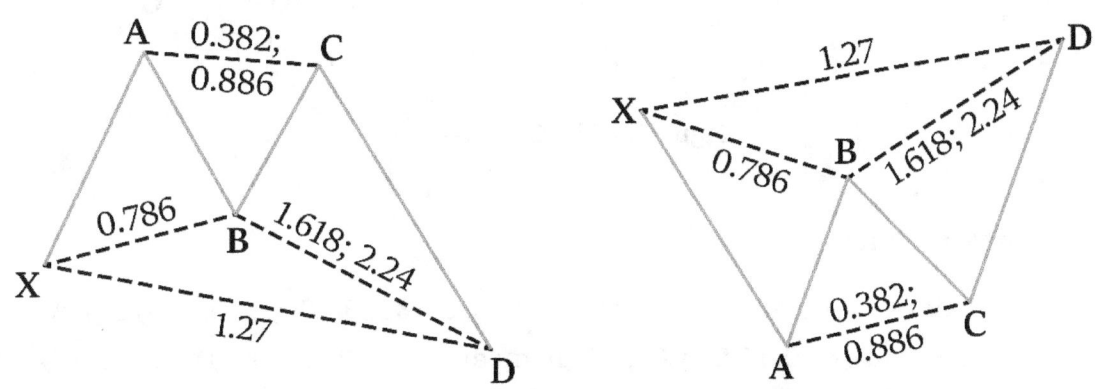

Figure 8 - The Butterfly pattern

The pattern structure:

- ✓ <u>B = 0.786 of XA</u>;
- ✓ C = from 0,382 to 0,886 (it means: 0.382, 0.500, 0.618, 0.707, 0.786, or 0.886) of AB (better from 0.618 to 0.886);
- ✓ D = from 1.618 to 2.24 (it means: 1.618, 2.000, or 2.240) of BC (ideal 1.618);
- ✓ D = from 1.272 to 1,618 (it means: 1.272, 1.414, or 1.618 of XA (ideal 1.272).

One of the most important ratios to define this pattern is the 0.786 retracement of XA since point B is one of the distinctive elements of the Butterfly pattern, and is essential for identifying point D. In a certain sense, the Butterfly is very similar to the Gartley pattern as it needs a well-defined point B.

• Like the Bat pattern, the **Crab** pattern was also created in 2000 by Scott Carney. Contrary to the Bat and Gartley patterns, this is not a corrective pattern. That is, ideally, you do not find it within corrective movements, but in the presence of impulsive movements.

It is characterised by a strong final movement, so much so that the projection of

BC can reach 3,618.

In figure 9, the Crab pattern, alongside all the Fibonacci calculations.

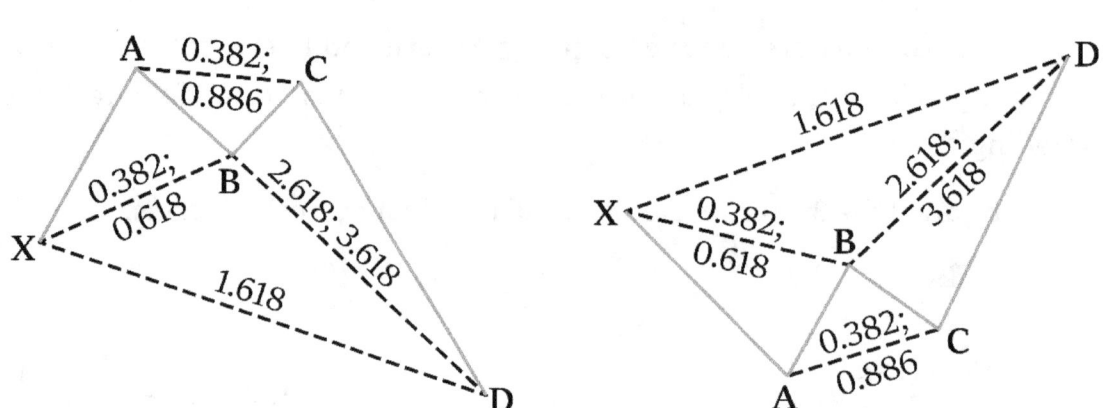

Figure 9 - The Crab pattern

Pattern structure:

- ✓ B = from 0.382 to 0.618 (it means: 0.382, 0.500, or 0.618) of XA;
- ✓ C = from 0.382 to 0.886 (it means: 0.382, 0.500, 0.618, 0.707, 0.786, or 0.886) of AB;
- ✓ D = <u>from 2,618 to 3,618</u> (it means: 2.618, 3.140, or 3.618) of BC;
- ✓ D = <u>max 1,618 of XA</u>.

The main characteristic that is taken into consideration for this pattern is the extension by 1,618 of the XA movement which determines point D. Together with the extreme projection of BC (2,618 - 3,14 - 3,618) they generate a valid area for the completion of the pattern.

The differences between the Butterfly and Crab patterns are several, although their structures may appear similar due to the fact that they are both "extension patterns." The Crab pattern uses a 1.618 extension of the XA leg, while the ideal Butterfly pattern has a 1.27 extension.

In the Butterfly pattern, point B has a 0.786 retracement of XA, while in the Crab pattern, it does not exceed 0.618. In short, the Butterfly pattern is characterised by a deeper retracement of point B than the Crab pattern and by a less significant extension of the XA leg to identify point D.

Now, to complete this chapter, let's take a look at how to calculate the various retracements/extensions on the chart. It is very simple. Every platform has the function to draw

Fibonacci retracements.

Below in figure 10, you can see the Usd-Jpy chart. First, you have to calculate the retracement of point B, the one that will define the type of pattern. It is simple; you have to click on the Fibonacci retracement icon on the platform, then click on point X and again on point A (or on another point on the chart but at the same height as point A).

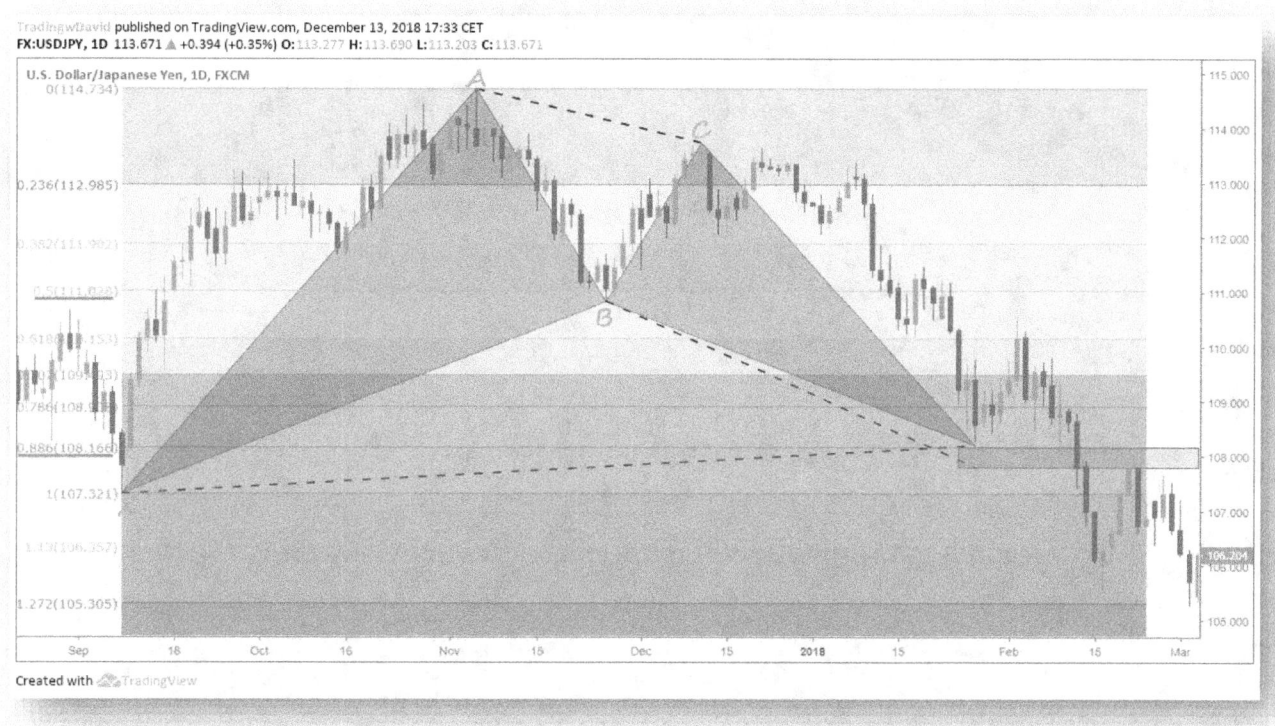

Figure 10 – Usd-Jpy, B point retracement (TradingView.com)

As you can see, point B has retraced about 0.500 of the movement that from X has brought the price to A. Retracements rarely stop exactly on a Fibonacci ratio, what is crucial is that it doesn't deviate much.

Once you have calculated the retracement of point B, with the same chart above you can calculate point D, as retracement (in this case) or extension of XA. Point B retracement (0.500) has defined the pattern, a Bat, so D = 0.886 of XA.

You are most likely thinking: "hey, Crab patterns also have the same retracement points." You are right, but as you will see explained in the next chapter, I only use the Crab as a final target.

Now you have to calculate the retracement of point C. The process is the same used previously and that you can see in figure 11. In this case, point C has a retracement of about 0.707 of AB.

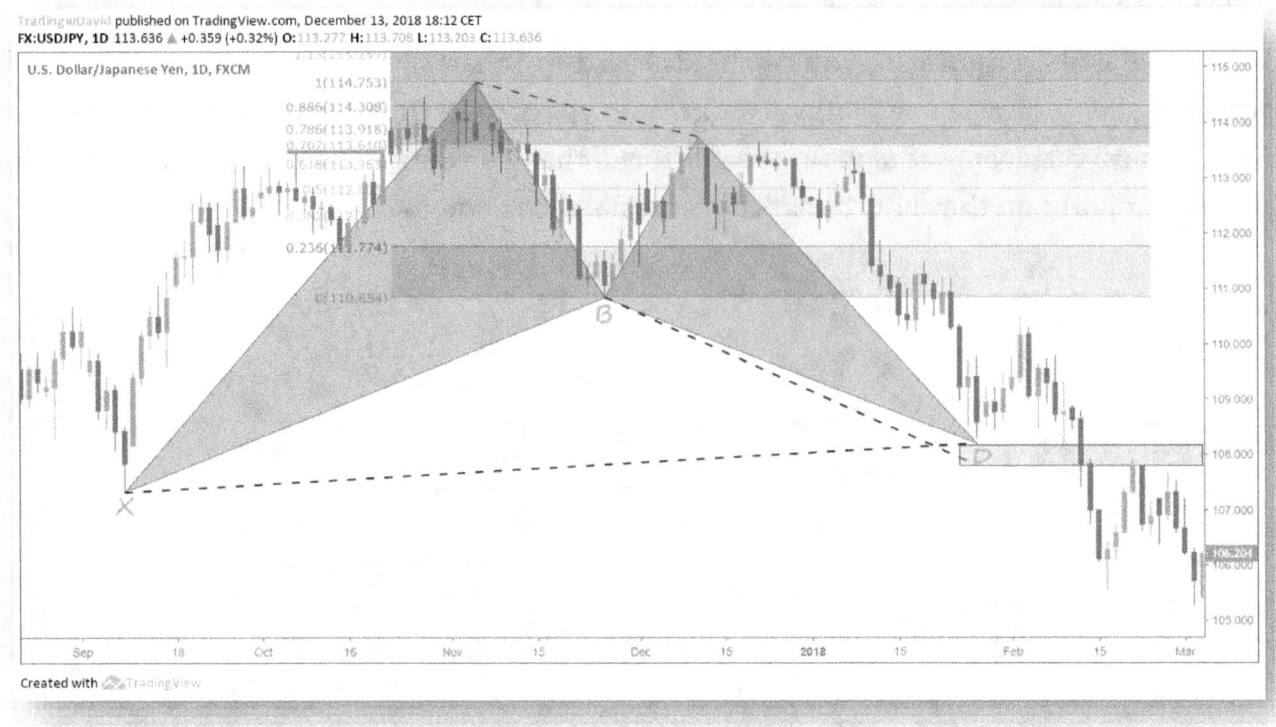

Figure 11 - Usd-Jpy, C point retracement (TradingView.com)

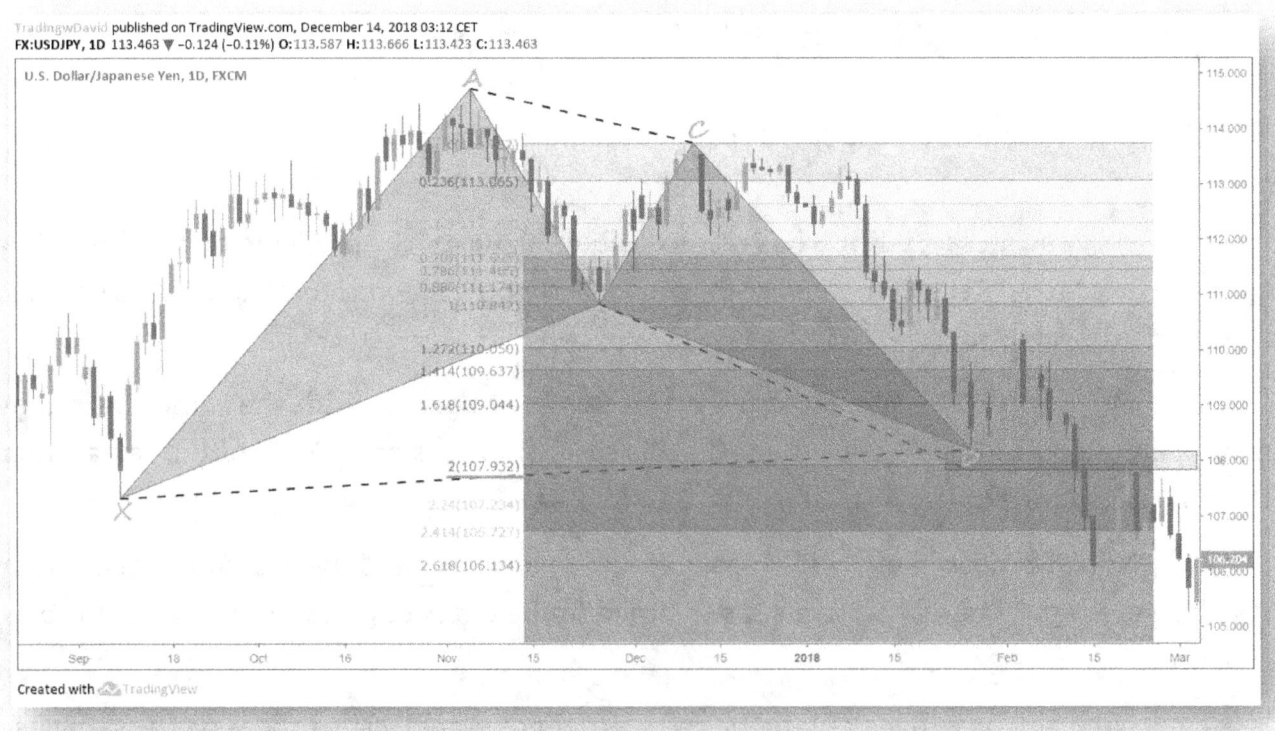

Figure 12 - Usd-Jpy, D point retracement (TradingView.com)

Point C in my strategy is important because I have noticed, especially in Forex, that the deeper the retracement of point C, the greater the chances that the price will reach the target.

Lastly, you have seen that point D as an extension of BC can be 1.618, 2.000, 2.240 or 2.618. As you can see in the chart in figure 12 above, in this case it is 2.000, and it is used as the target area (I will explain target and stop-loss in more detail in the next chapter).

What you very briefly saw in this chapter were the four Harmonic Patterns that I exploit in my strategy, but used in a different way to their classical use. Indeed, I do not look for potential turning points in the market, but patterns of continuation of a movement, with a well-defined target area.

I am going to explain my strategy step by step in the next chapter.

The Strategy

CHAPTER 2

The strategy I am going to explain is based on Harmonic Patterns. Four of them, to be precise. The strategy, at first sight, may seem complex, but in the end, you will see that it is easy to apply.

I closed the previous chapter by saying that I like to exploit Harmonic Patterns in my strategy, but in a way that varies from their classical use. I do not seek potential turning points in the market, but patterns of continuation of a movement, with a well-defined target area.

What does this mean? Harmonic Patterns are reversal patterns. The completion of a Harmonic Pattern identifies a Potential Reversal Zone (PRZ) where price is very likely to rebound or reverse. The PRZ is a zone around point D (but I will not explain exactly how to identify it).

What I do with my strategy is, once points B and C are defined, I try to ride the last leg (from point C to point D), that will most likely bring the price to the completion of the Harmonic Pattern identified by point B.

Do not worry. I will give you plenty of examples in order for you to properly understand this strategy and all its parameters. But let's start immediately with the first example.

In figure 13 you can see the Eur-Aud daily chart.

In the last month, the currency pair has fallen. By applying my strategy, it would have been possible to get a significant profit.

There is one more thing that I want to make clear before starting to explain the strategy. The examples I use to explain these concepts do not reflect "trading with hindsight." They are all trades I have done on my trading account, with real money, and that I posted on my TradingView page, at the time when the signal was completed.

Figure 13 - Eur-Aud daily chart (TradingView.com)

Figure 14 - Eur-Aud daily chart (TradingView.com)

Look at the same chart, but now with some trendlines (figure 14 above).

Now on the chart you can now see something slightly more familiar. What is forming is a Bullish Bat pattern. It is not completed yet, therefore, it has not given a bullish signal, but, as I have already mentioned, this is not the kind of signal I am seeking.

What is my idea? Try to ride the last leg of the Bat pattern, the one that leads the price from point C to point D. But how? Simply by opening a short trade after the breakout of the black trendline, that is, the line that starts from X and passes from point B.

What do I mean when I say the "breakout of the black trendline?" Here, I will tell you right now: this aspect depends on you and your kind of trading. There are more or less aggressive strategies you can employ when entering a market.

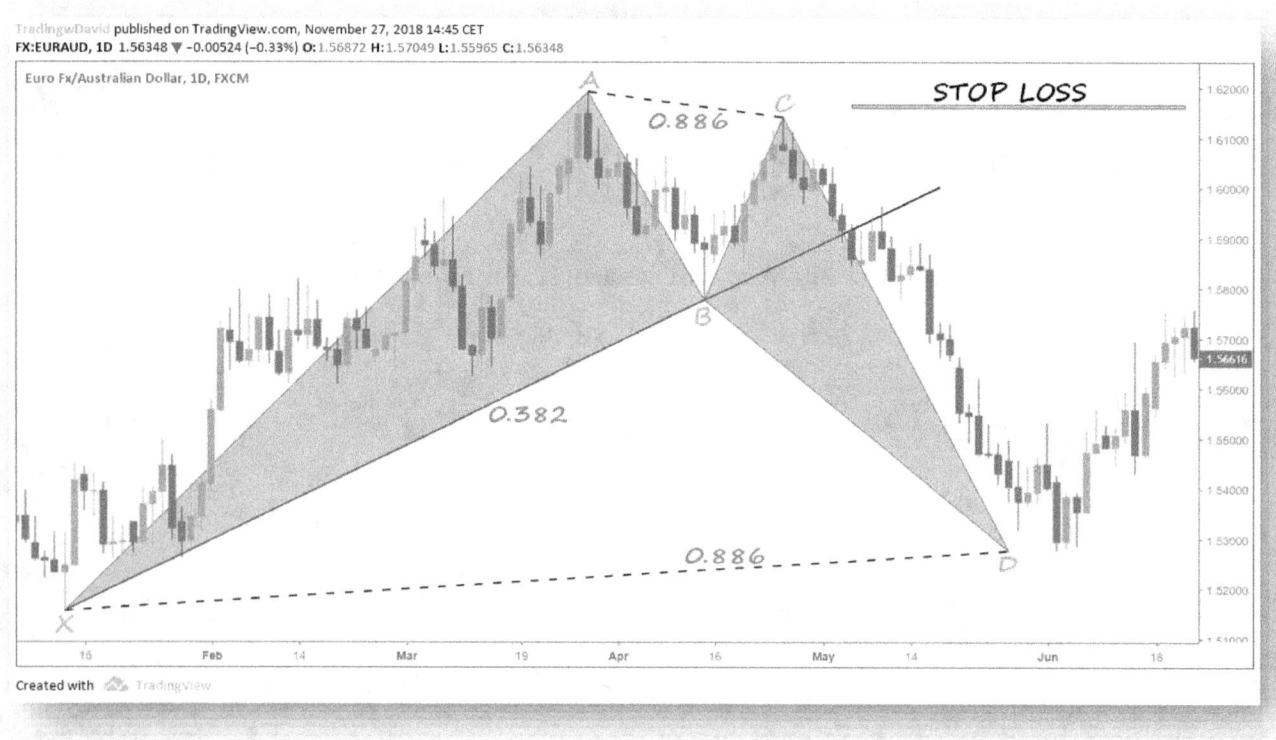

Figure 15 - Eur-Aud, stop-loss (TradingView.com)

The more aggressive method is to open a position when the price crosses the black trendline. In this way, doing this will mean definitely being inside the trade should it develop positively, but also means risking being a victim of a false breakout.

A less aggressive strategy is to wait for a close in price beyond the trendline before opening a trade. The entry price in the market will be worse, it will be lower than the more aggressive strategy seen above, but in this way, at least part the fakeouts will be avoided.

16

The less aggressive strategy, but that is likely to lose good trades, is to wait for a pullback in price on the black trendline that, as far as my experience has taught me, is not very rare to see. You will see this aspect in more detail in the next chapter. As I said, the choice of the moment in which to open a trade is up to you. You have to choose the type of trade entry that is best suited for your trading and personality. And what about the stop-loss and target? Let's take a look at them right now (figure 15 above).

Now the pattern on the chart is clear. It is, as mentioned, a Bullish Bat that is yet to be completed. It will be if the price reaches 1.52750 (point D), which is the target area of the short trade. I am talking about the "target area" because you have seen that there is another parameter in a Harmonic Pattern, CD as the extension of BC. I report below the one for the Bat pattern:

CD = from 1,618 to 2,618 (it means: 1.618, 2.000, 2.240, or 2.618) of BC

Now, look at this new Eur-Aud daily chart (figure 16).

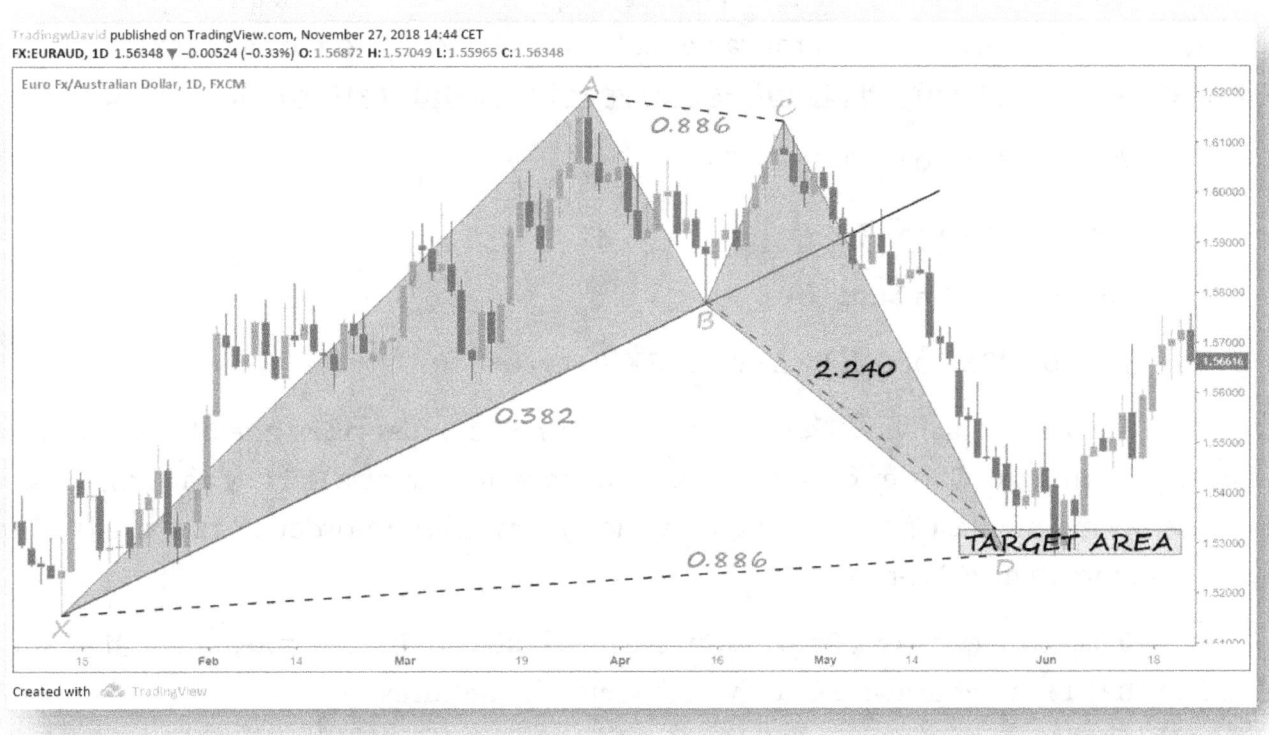

Figure 16 - Eur-Aud, the target area (TradingView.com)

Below, the two levels that have formed in the chart:

CD = 2.24BC = 1.5322

AD = 0.786XA = 1.5275

17

From this, it follows that the target area of the short trade on Eur-Aud is 1.5322/1.5275. A range of 53 pips within which to take profit. In the examples from this chapter, you have seen how this strategy almost always generates trades with an excellent risk/reward ratio. This allows you to do two things: move the stop at break-even after a certain gain, and close part of the position when the price reaches a certain level.

About the stop-loss: it has to be positioned beyond point C. I usually put it at a distance of 20/25 pips/ticks from it (you always have to consider that these are trades on a daily chart). Even here, everyone can decide differently. The important thing is to always insert the stop-loss and open an appropriate position size according to your account (as I will demonstrate better in the sixth chapter of this book).

With this first example, you have seen the idea which is at the basis of this strategy: to exploit a probable completion of a harmonic pattern. You have figured out how the signal is generated, where to place the stop-loss, and how to calculate the target area.

This is a strategy that, if correctly applied, with an adequate position size, generates a very high percentage of profitable trades. I draw inspiration from the example above to repeat a basic concept. **Point B identifies the type of harmonic pattern**. More precisely:

AB = 0.382XA or 0.500XA = Bat

AB = 0.618XA = Gartley

AB = 0.786XA = Butterfly

AB = 0.382XA or 0.500XA or 0.618XA = Crab

I work in this way. The retracement of point B identifies one of the first three Harmonic patterns (Bat, Gartley or Butterfly). In the case of a Bat or a Gartley pattern, the Crab gives me a second and last potential target, which I leave free in order to run a part of my position (no more than 20% of it).

The completion of a Crab requires a deep bullish or bearish movement. It does not occur often that a market draws a Crab (which generally requires several weeks to complete). But when this happens, I assure you that the satisfaction of having ridden that big movement is priceless.

Let's move onto another aspect. It may happen that on a chart, depending on the X point, there is more than one Harmonic pattern. In this case, how should you behave? Let's take a look at this situation using an example.

In figures 17 and 18 below, you can see the same Nikkei daily chart with two different Harmonic patterns, a Bat pattern (in blue) and a Gartley pattern (in yellow).

Figure 17 - Nikkei, Bearish Bat (TradingView.com)

Figure 18 - Nikkei, Bearish Gartley (TradingView.com)

So, in this case, you have two different Harmonic Patterns in the same chart. Which of the two do you have to take into account? The Bat or the Gartley?

This is how I think, but no one is preventing you from doing differently; it is far better to adapt a strategy to your own style of trading than copying the decisions of another trader, with another trading style. I take as my main pattern the larger one (in this case the Bat) and use the "narrower" pattern (the Gartley) to close part of the position.

In practice, the two Harmonic patterns give me two D points. I consider point D formed by the Bat (the widest pattern) as the target area, and the one generated by the Gartley (the narrower pattern) as an area where I can close half or part of the position. Below are the Harmonic patterns for Nikkei (figure 19).

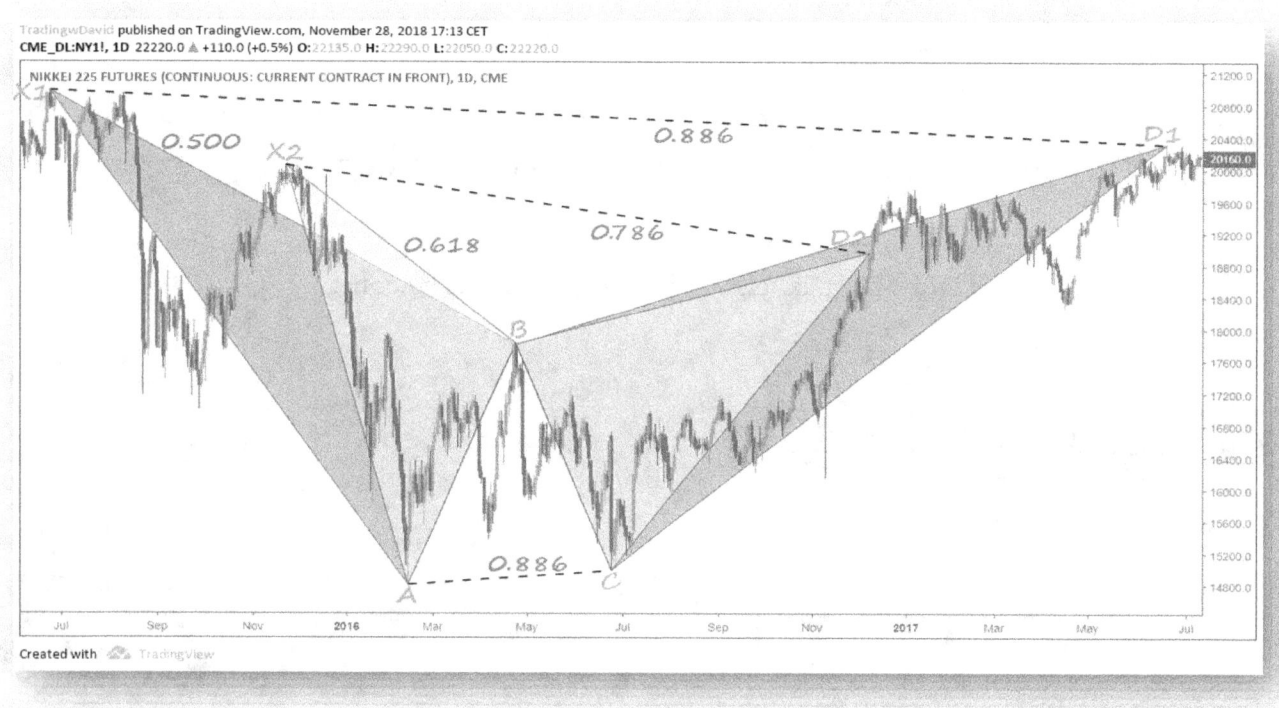

Figure 19 - Nikkei futures (TradingView.com)

When the price reaches point D2, I close part of the trade, going on to close the whole position once it reaches point D1. But look at the chart in figure 20. A Crab as I said before, can bring great satisfaction and a little part of the trade should always be left free to ride a possible completion of this pattern.

One final consideration concerning this type of situation. I always use, as a trading signal, the breakout of the line that starts from X1 and passes from B. So, the line of the larger pattern (the Bat in the Nikkei chart). Again, no one prevents you from doing the opposite.

Figure 20 - Nikkei futures, Bearish Crab (TradingView.com)

Figure 21 - Nzd-Usd, Bullish Bat (TradingView.com)

In this first part of the chapter, I explained the strategy; now you know how it works and how to use it. In this second part, I will show several examples that will demonstrate how much it can be profitable (with a very high percentage of successful trades). But before, I want to specify that a high percentage does not mean 100% profit, rather, sometimes it can happen that a trade is closed with the stop-loss having been hit by the price. You can see this particular situation in figure 21 above with the Nzd-Usd daily chart.

The above is a trade I did a few months prior to writing this chapter, and that left a bitter taste in my mouth. First, the price hits my stop-loss, rising above point C, only to then collapse, reaching the target area. Unfortunately, these are situations that can happen, and you have to accept them. Another consideration. You know that windows (gaps) in Forex are rare and can be formed only between the Friday close and Sunday open. In the stock market, they happen much more often. You only look at what happens on a chart the day after the release of the earnings.

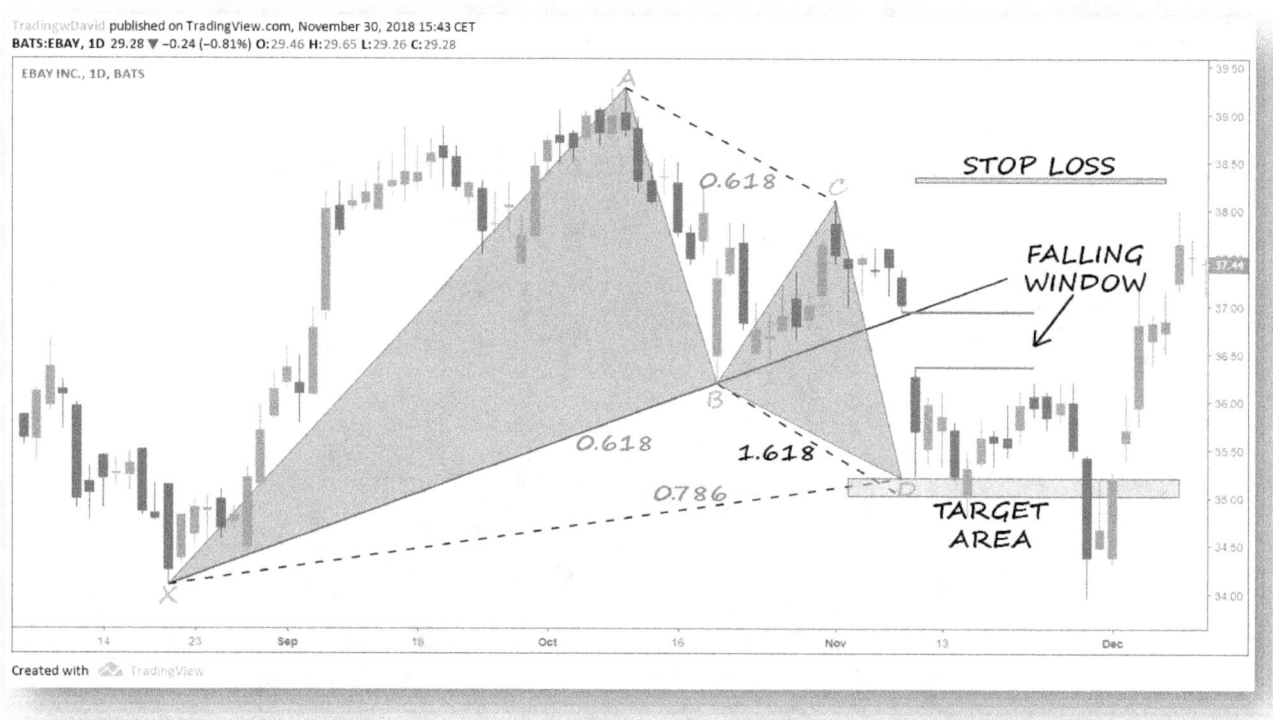

Figure 22 - eBay, Bullish Gartley (TradingView.com)

But how should you behave when, as in the eBay chart in figure 22 above, the black tendline is crossed with a gap? The price has to cross the black trendline, not jump it. However, after a window, you can wait and see if, after a few days, a close in the gap or pullback in price occurs on the black trendline (you will see more about pullbacks in the next chapter).

Now, let me give you a rundown of other examples. After this, I will reflect on some considerations made from my experiences using this strategy. Let's start with a Bearish Butterfly on the Eur-Usd daily chart (figure 23).

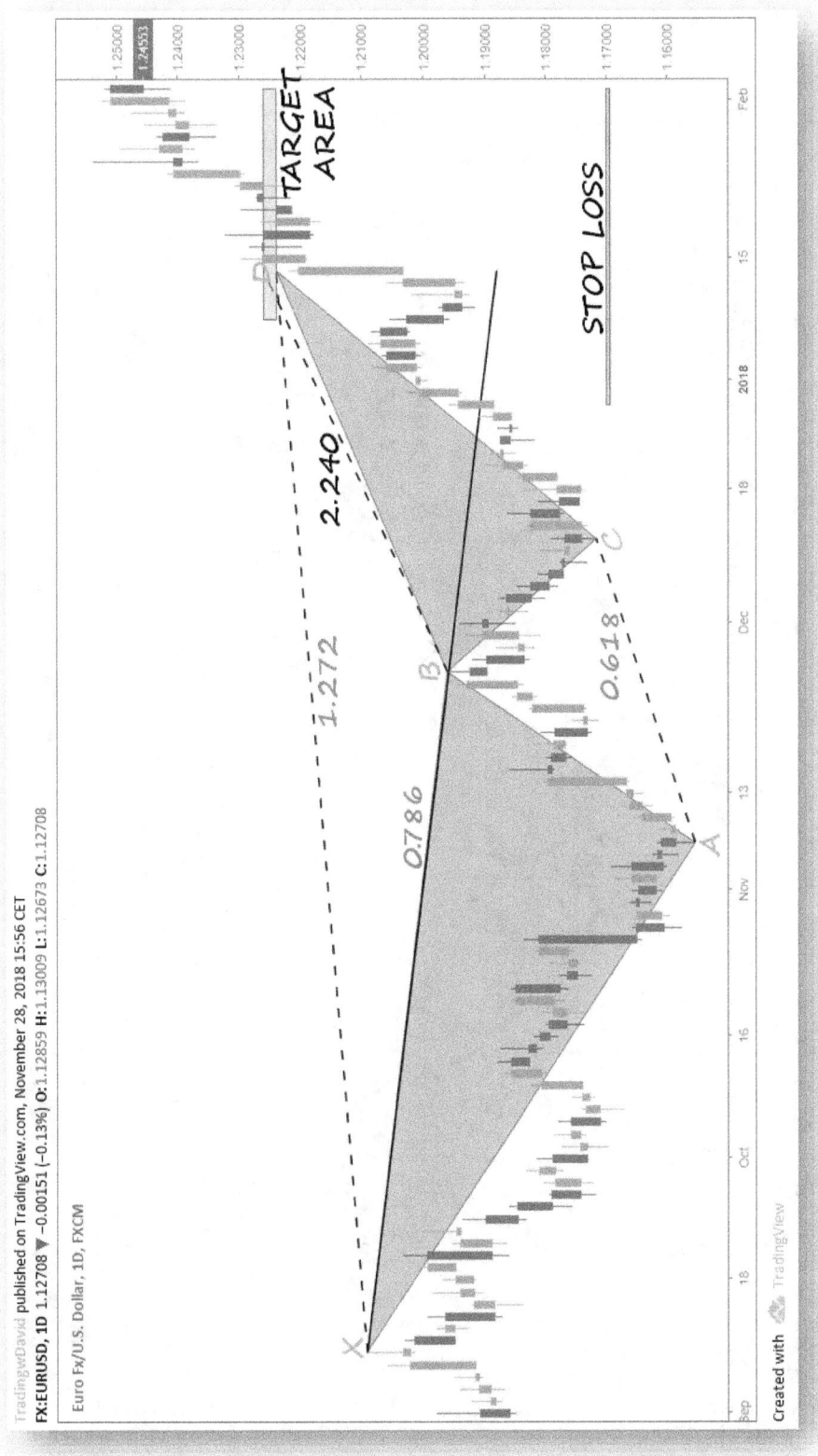

Figure 23 - Eur-Usd, Bearish Butterfly (TradingView.com)

A Bullish Bat on IBM chart in figure 24.

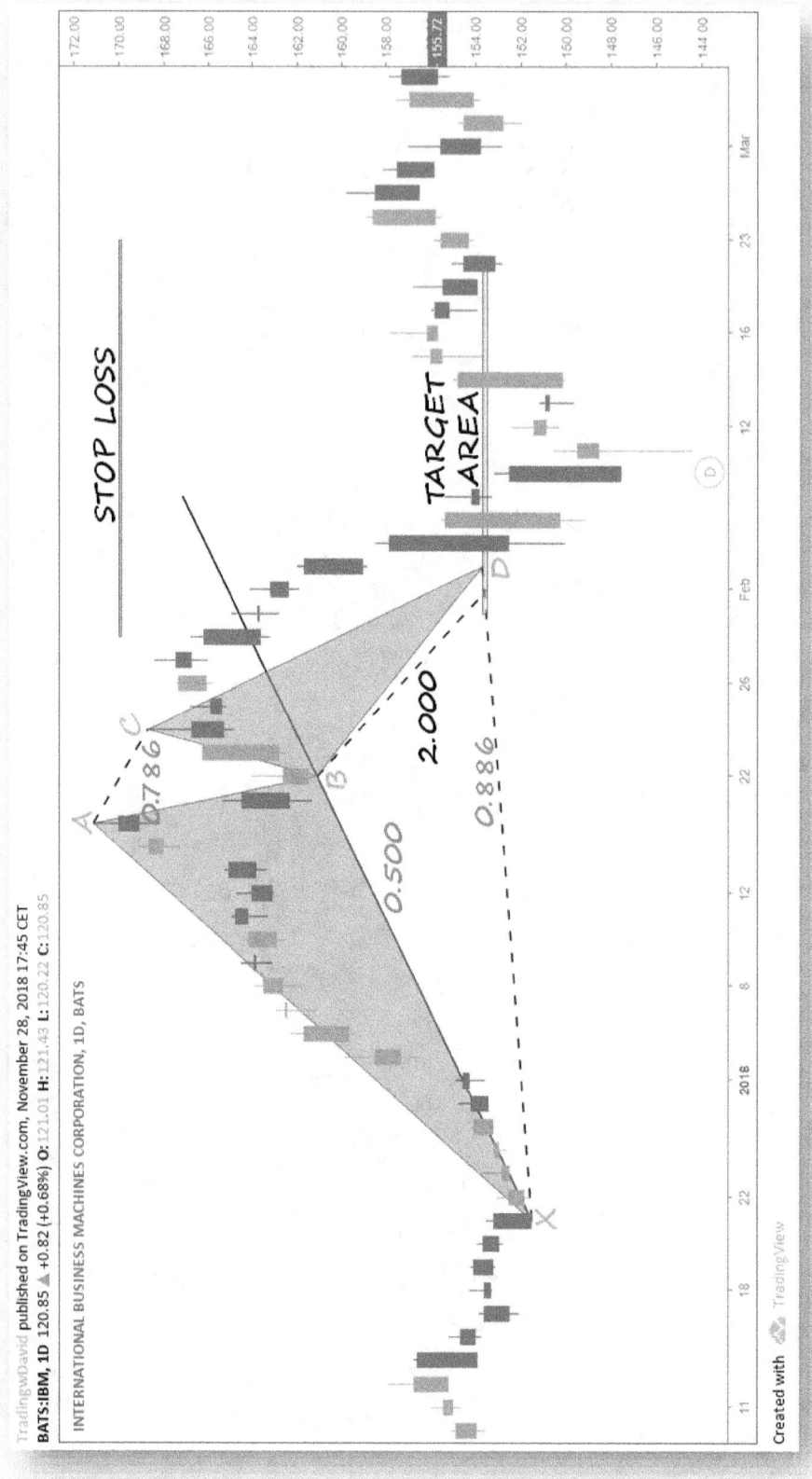

Figure 24 - IBM, Bullish Bat (TradingView.com)

A Bullish Bat on Usd-Chf daily chart in figure 25.

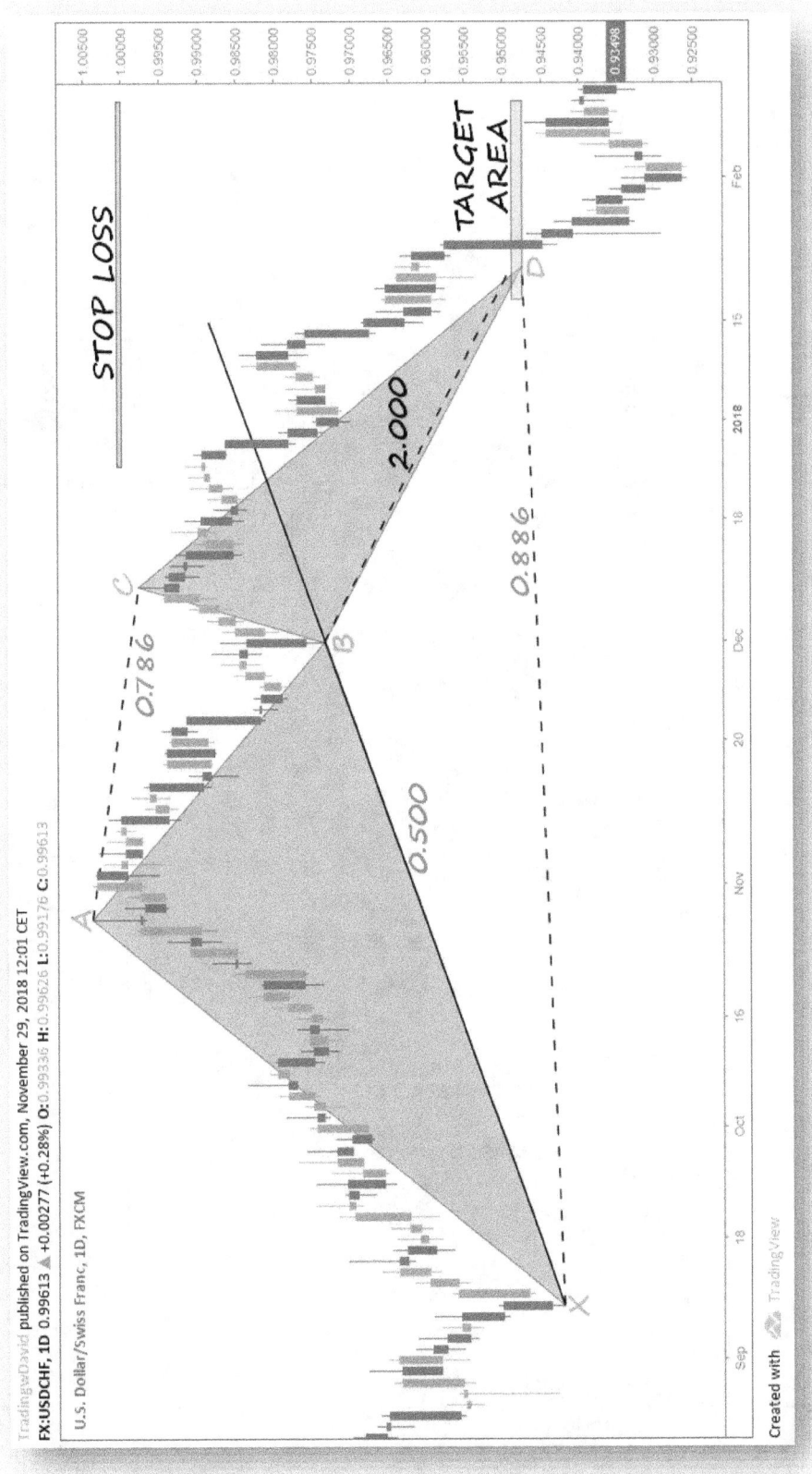

Figure 25 - Usd-Chf, Bullish Bat (TradingView.com)

A Bullish Gartley on United Technologies daily chart in figure 26.

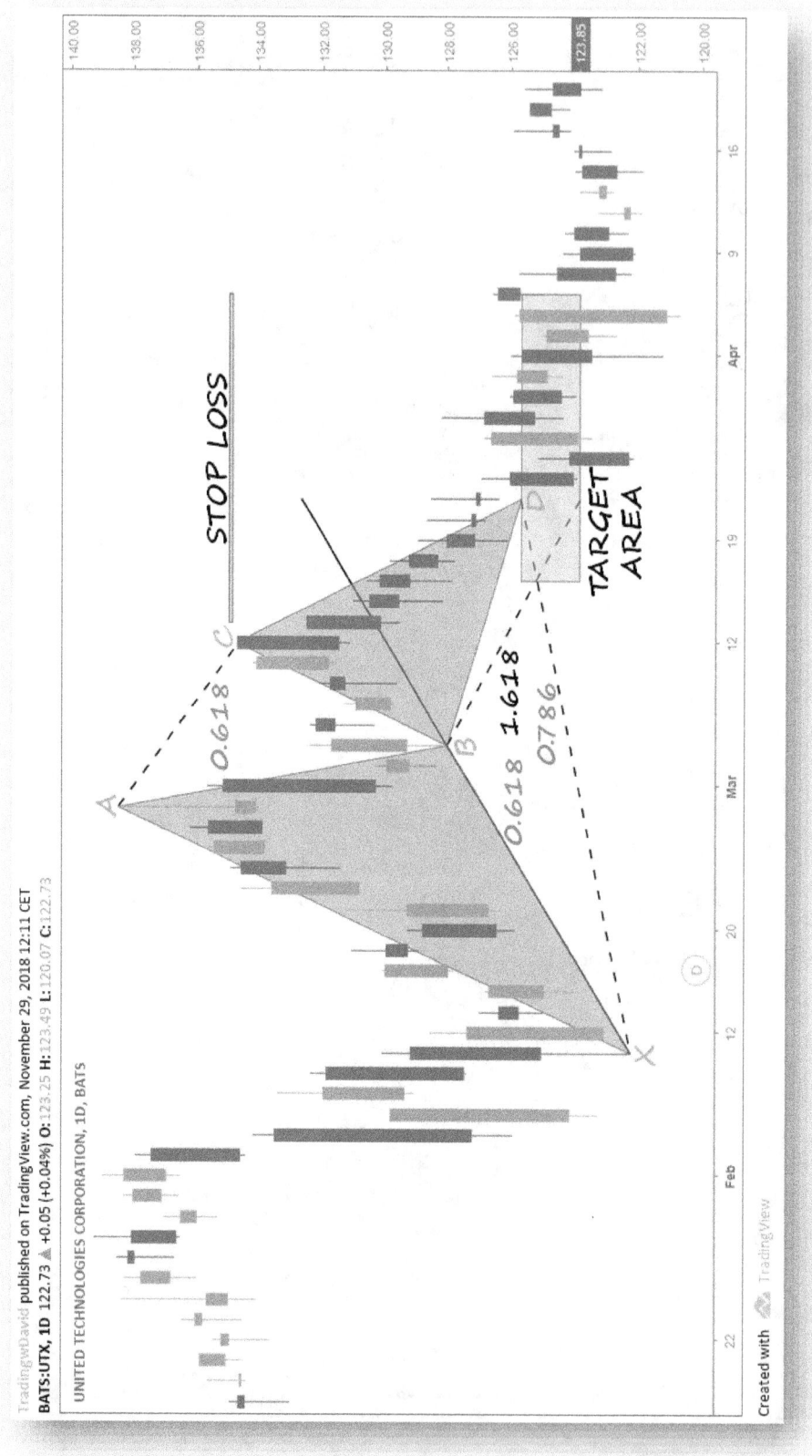

Figure 26 - United Technologies, Bullish Gartley (TradingView.com)

A Bearish Gartley on the Nasdaq100 daily chart in figure 27.

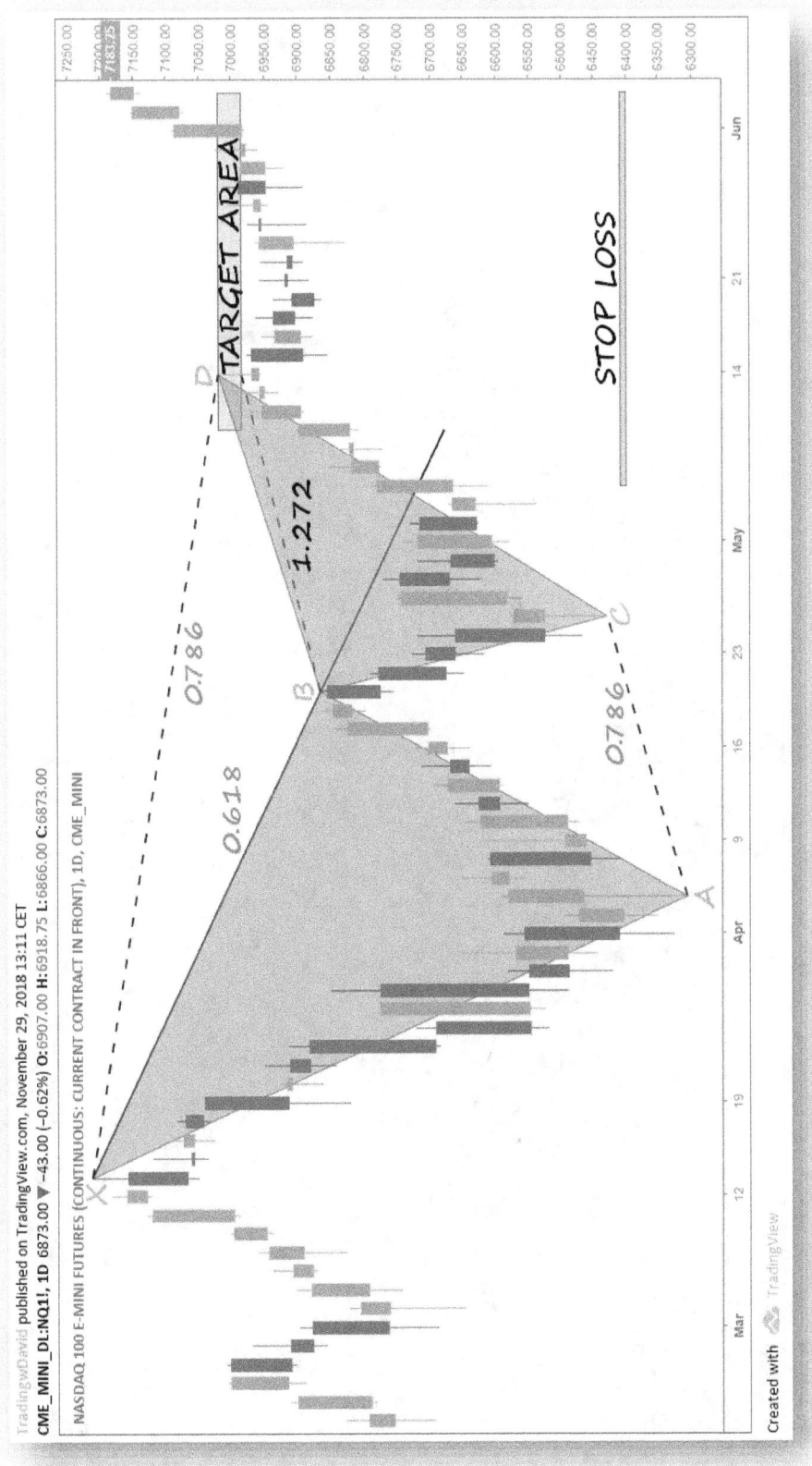

Figure 27 - Nasdaq100 futures, Bearish Gartley (TradingView.com)

A Bearish Gartley on Eur-Chf daily chart in figure 28.

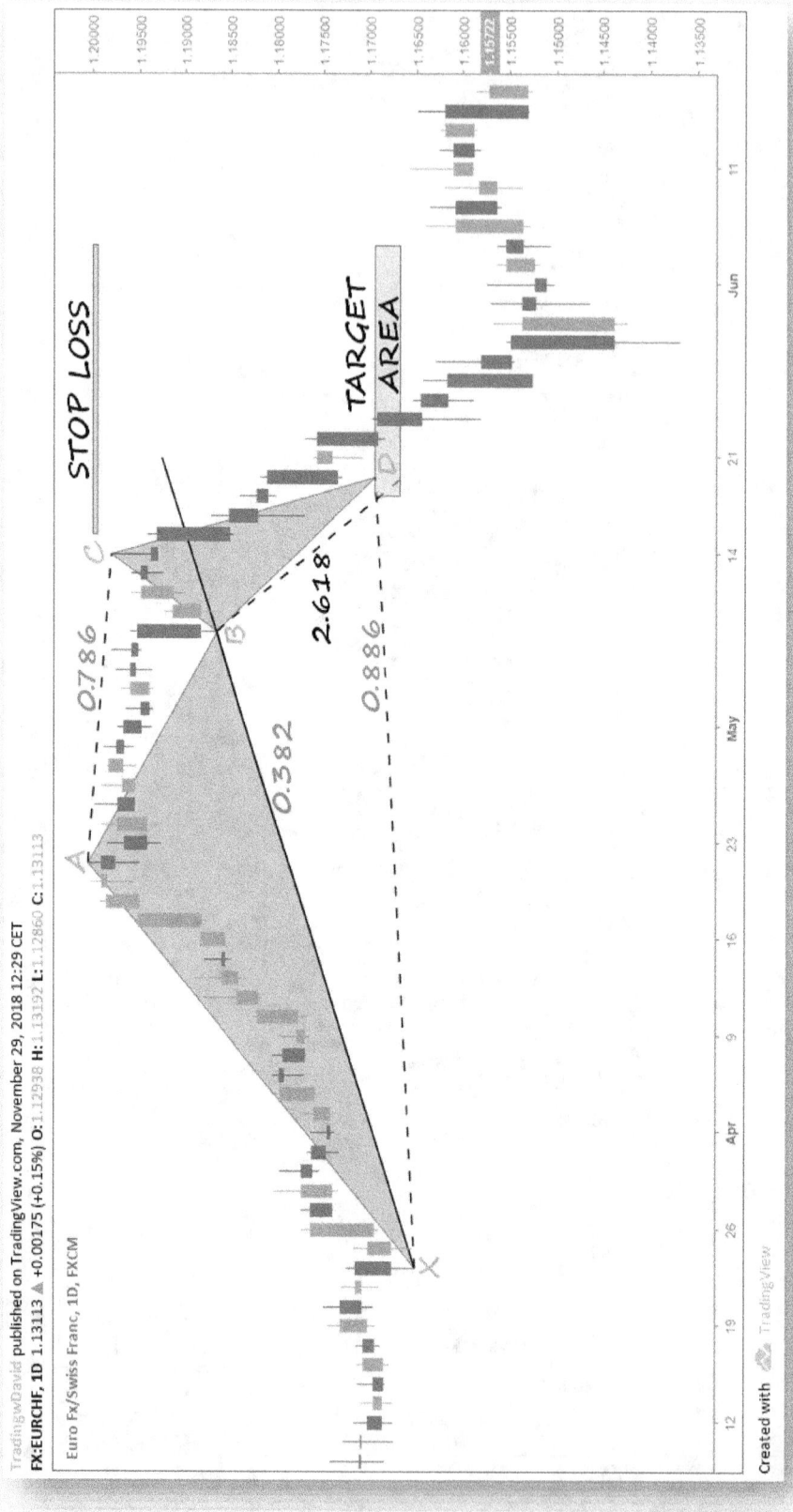

Figure 28 - Eur-Chf, Bullish Bat (TradingView.com)

A Bearish Butterfly on Natural Gas daily chart in figure 29.

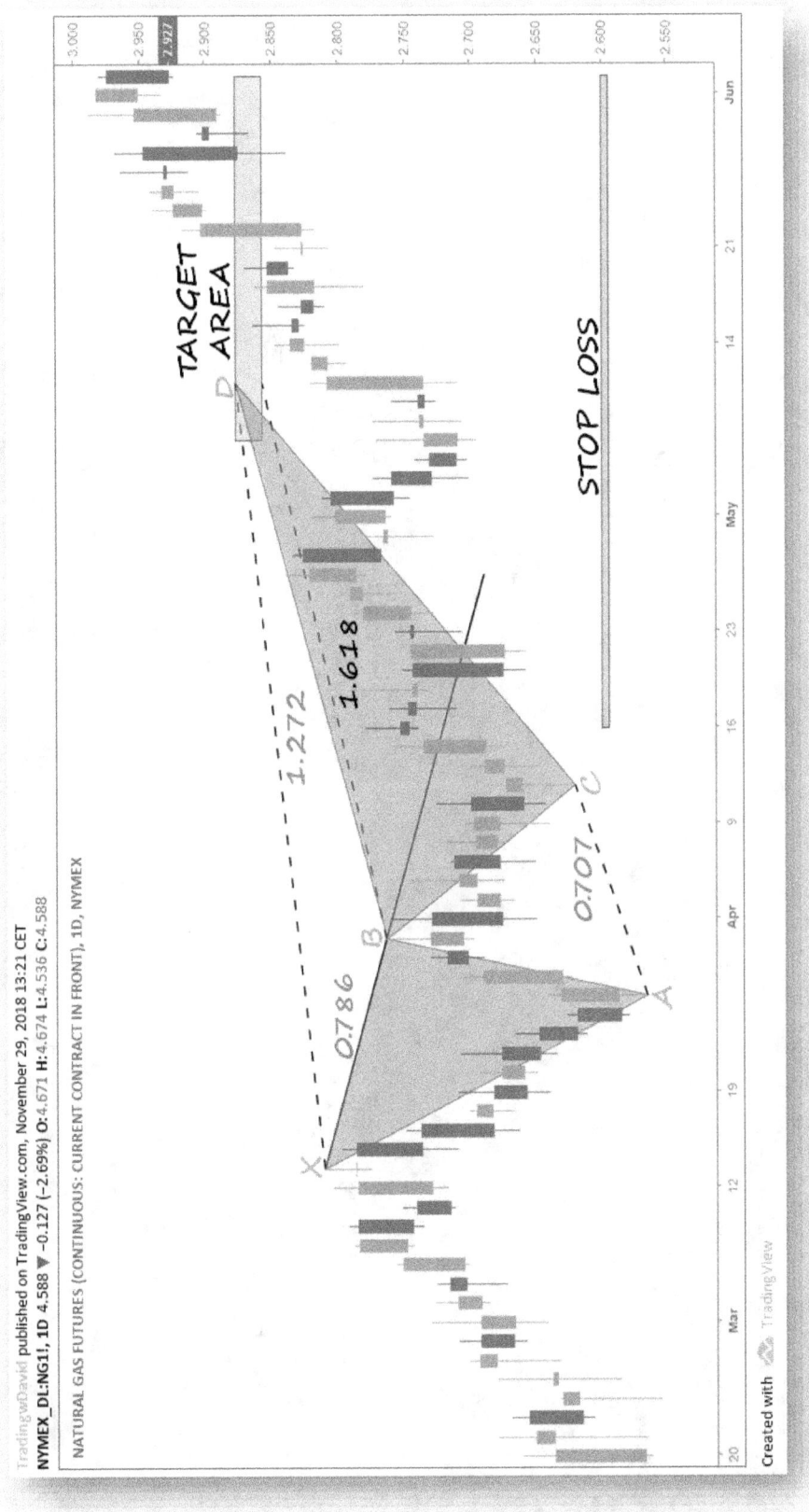

Figure 29 - Natural Gas, Bearish Butterfly (TradingView.com)

A Bullish Gartley on Aud-Usd daily chart in figure 30.

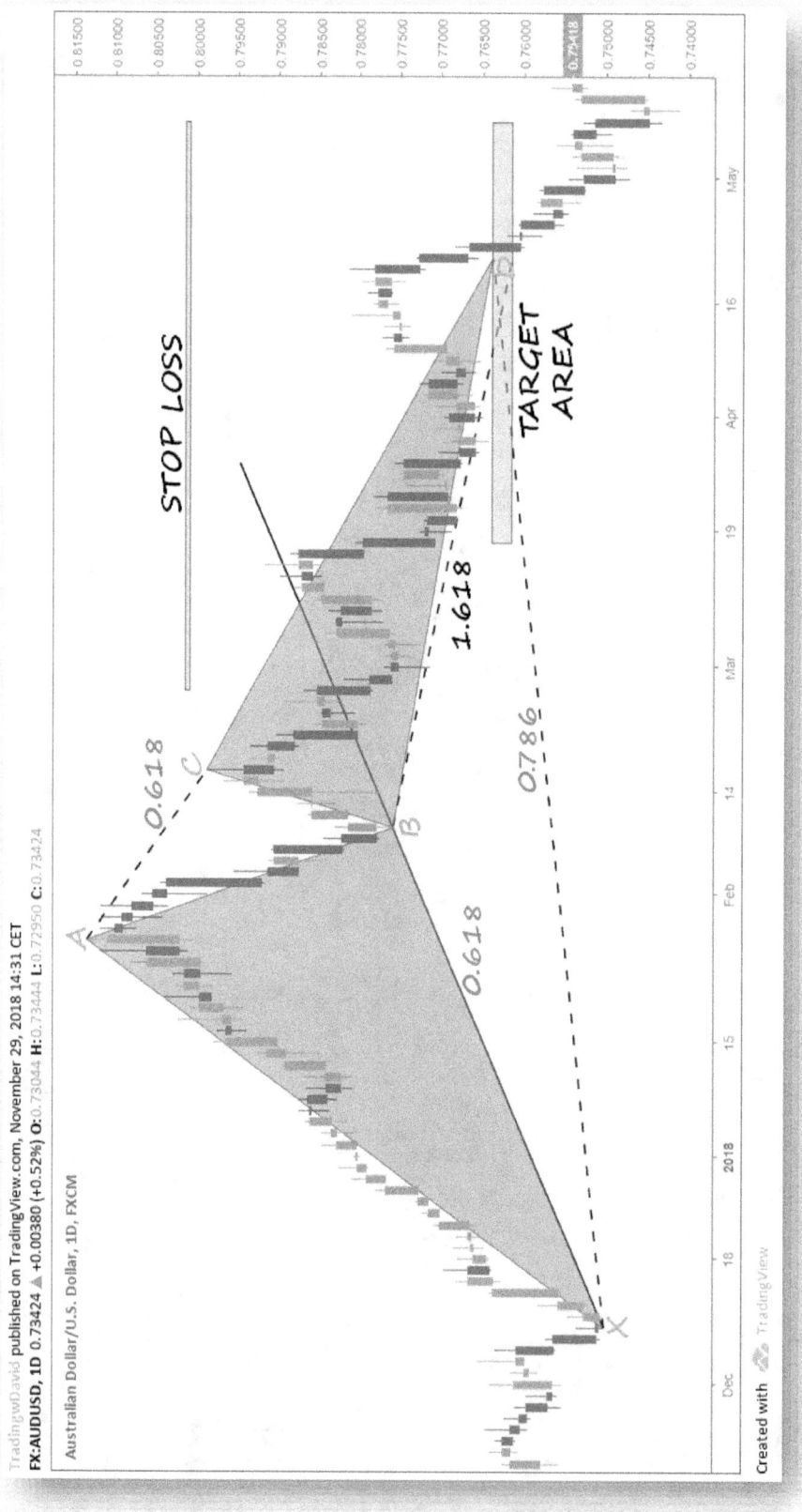

Figure 30 - Aud-Usd, Bullish Gartley (TradingView.com)

A Bearish Butterfly on MasterCard daily chart in figure 31.

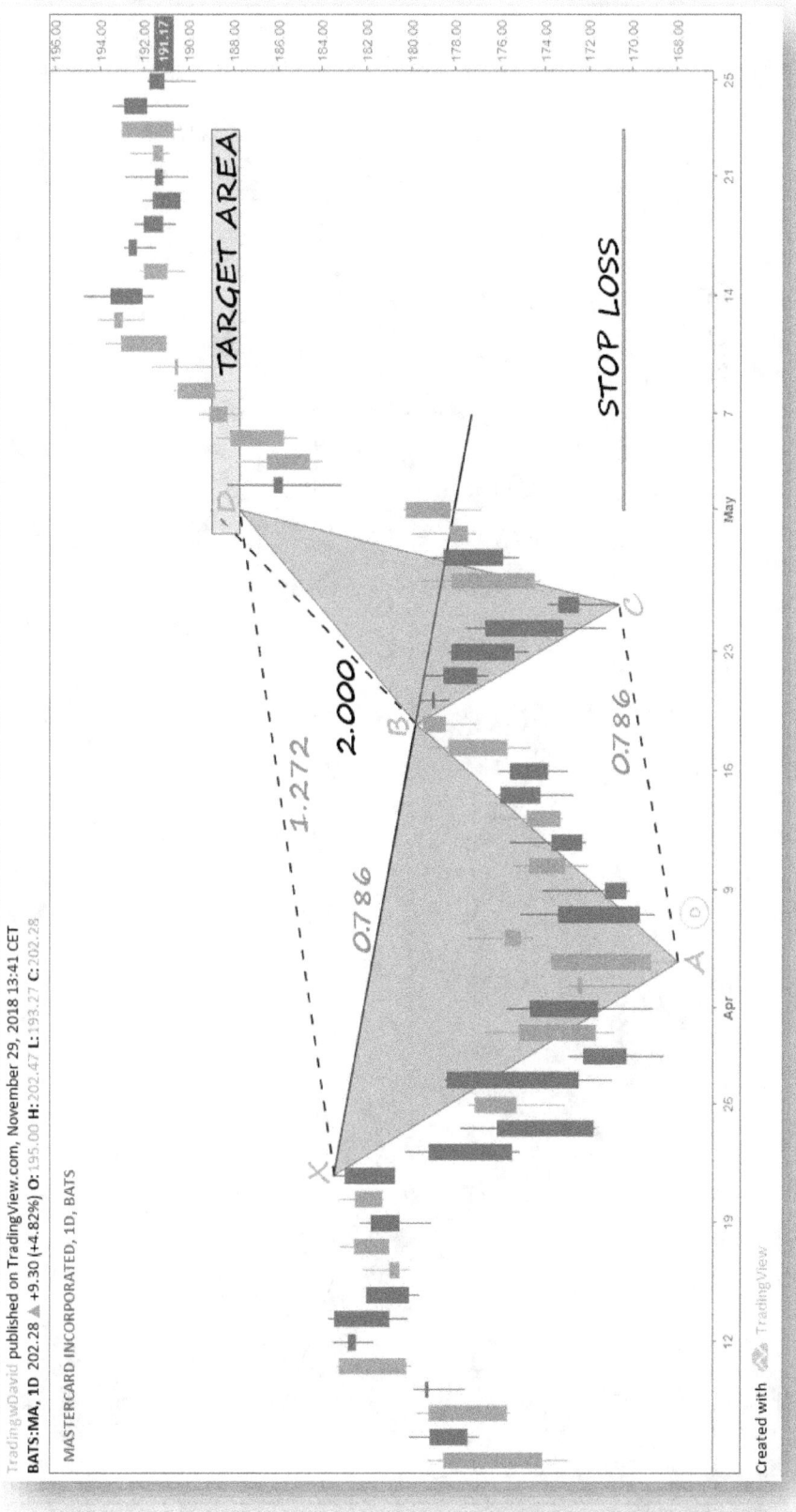

Figure 31 - MasterCard, Bearish Butterfly (TradingView.com)

A Bullish Bat on Usd-Jpy daily chart in figure 32.

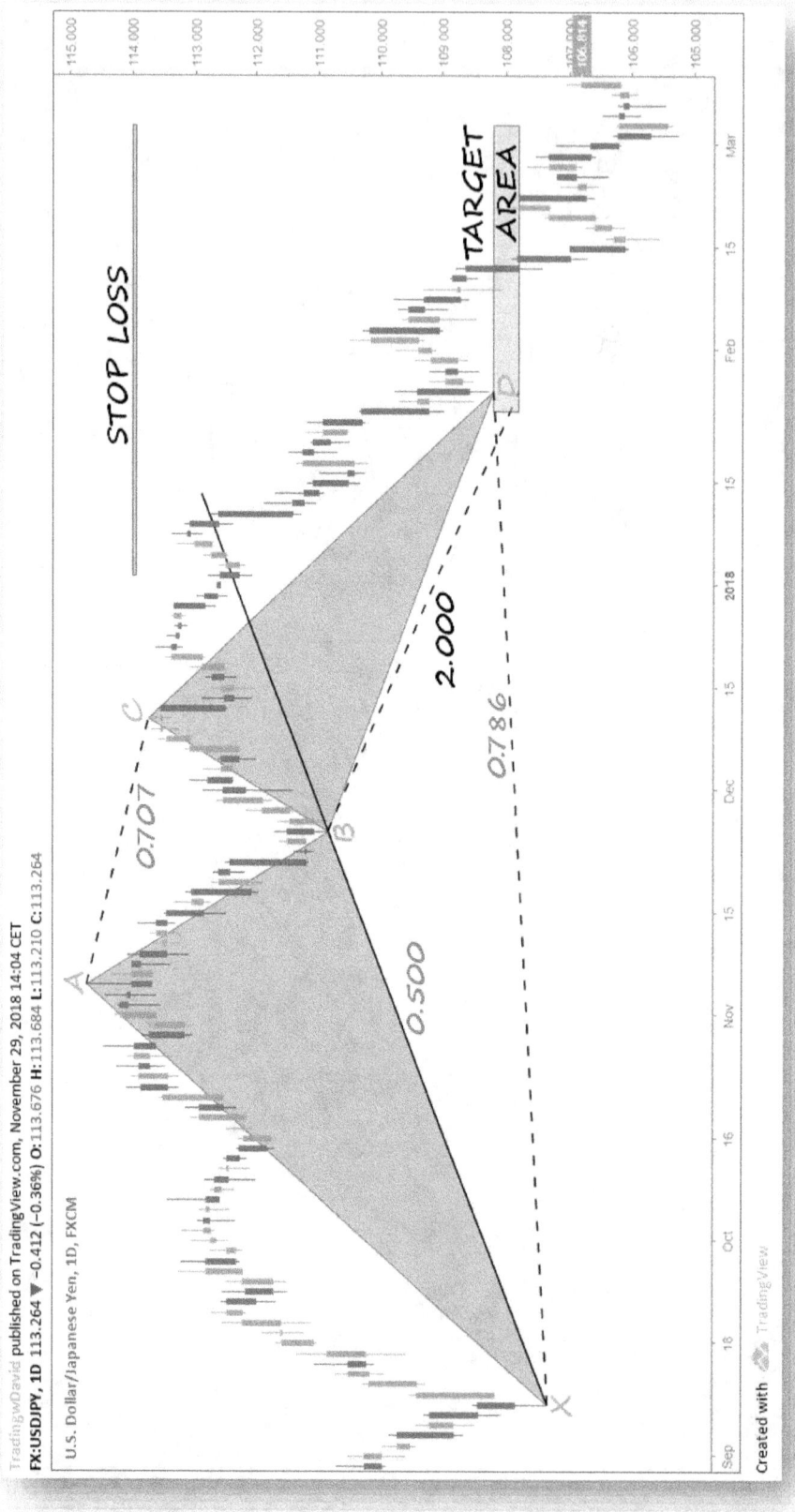

Figure 32 - Usd-Jpy, Bullish Bat (TradingView.com)

A Bearish Bat on Usd-Sek daily chart in figure 33.

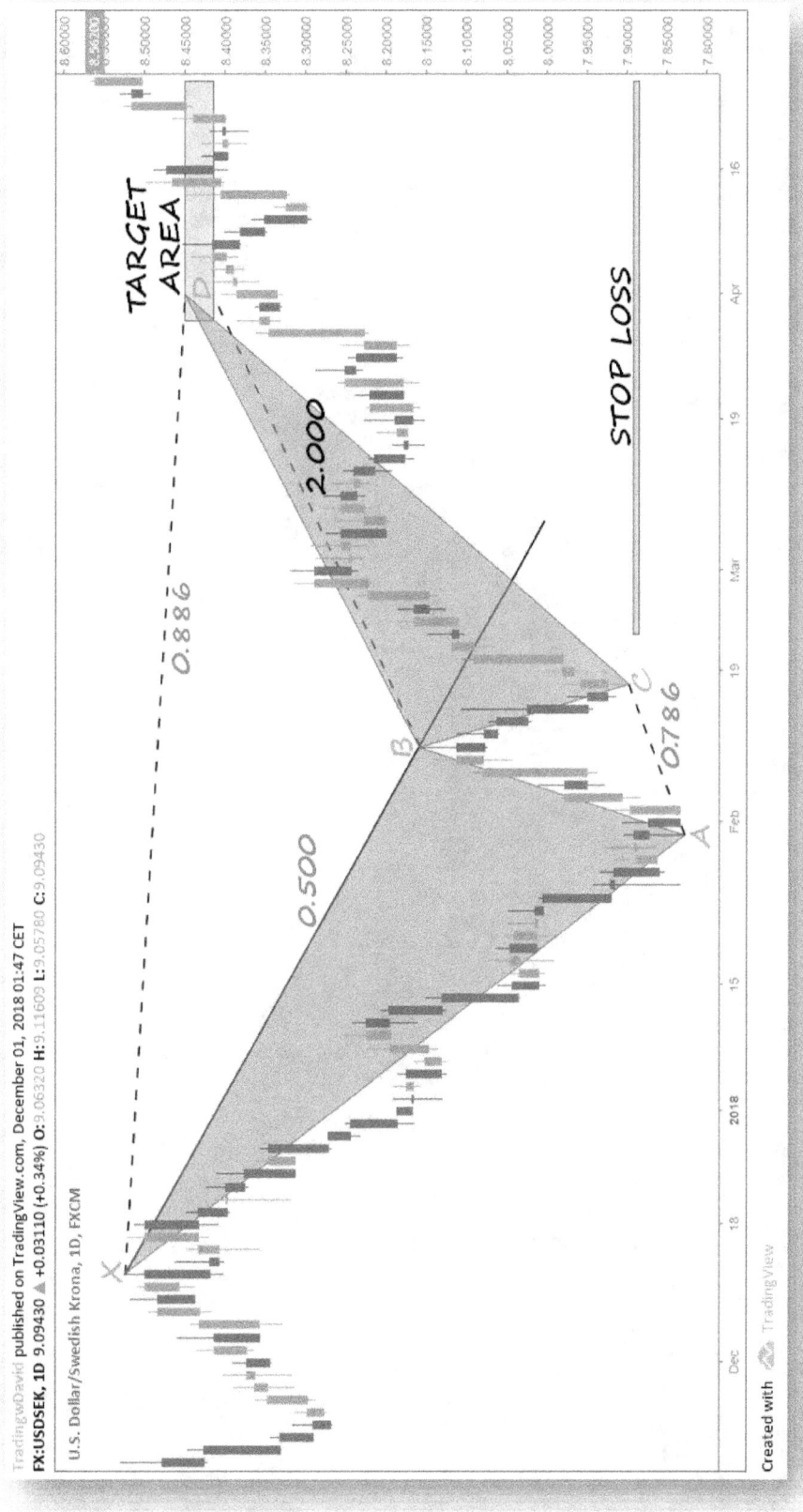

Figure 33 - Usd-Sek, Bearish Bat (TradingView.com)

A Bullish Bat on AUS200 daily chart in figure 34.

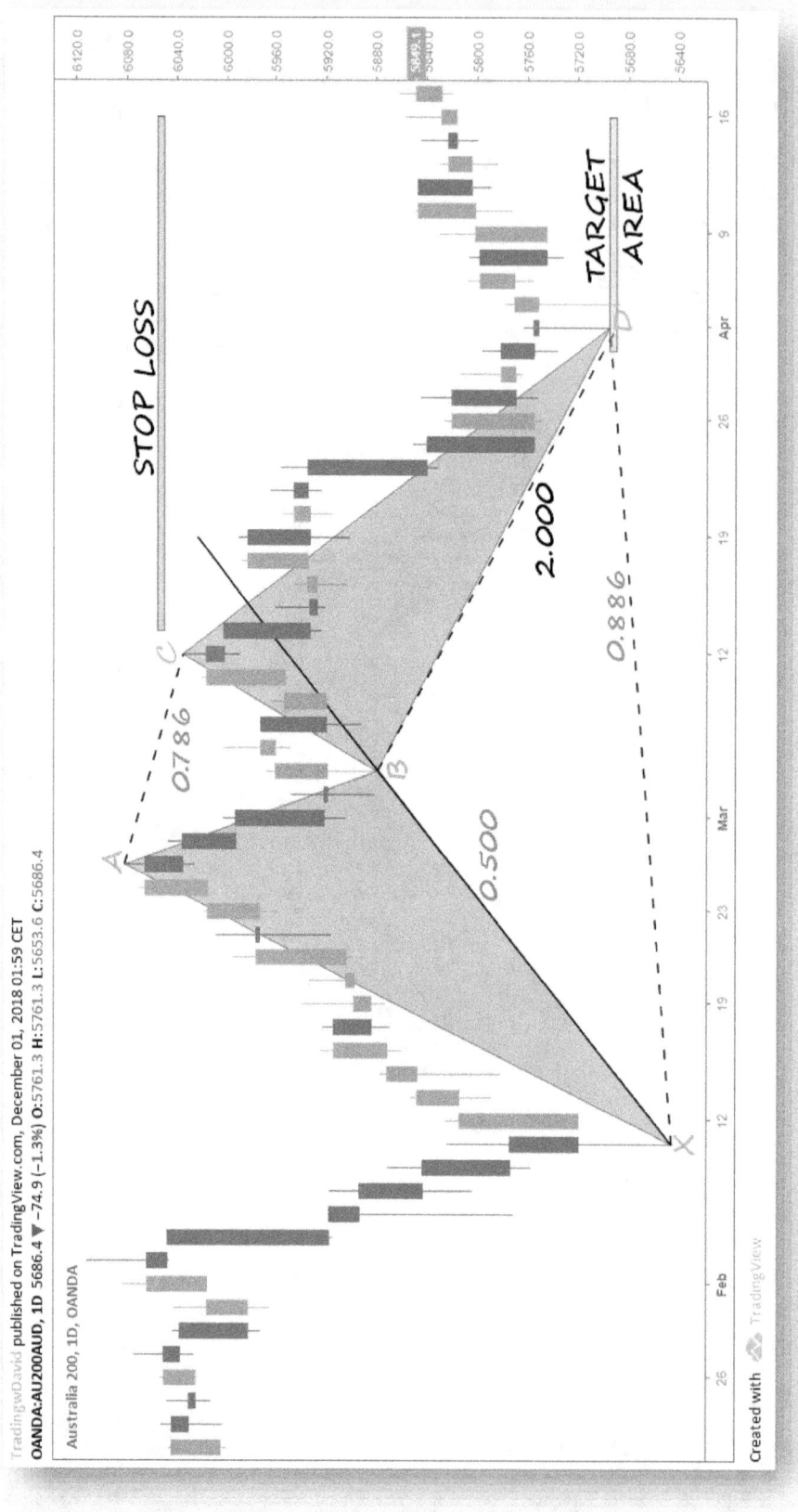

Figure 34 - AUS200, Bullish Bat (TradingView.com)

A Bearish Butterfly on Eur-Jpy weekly chart in figure 35.

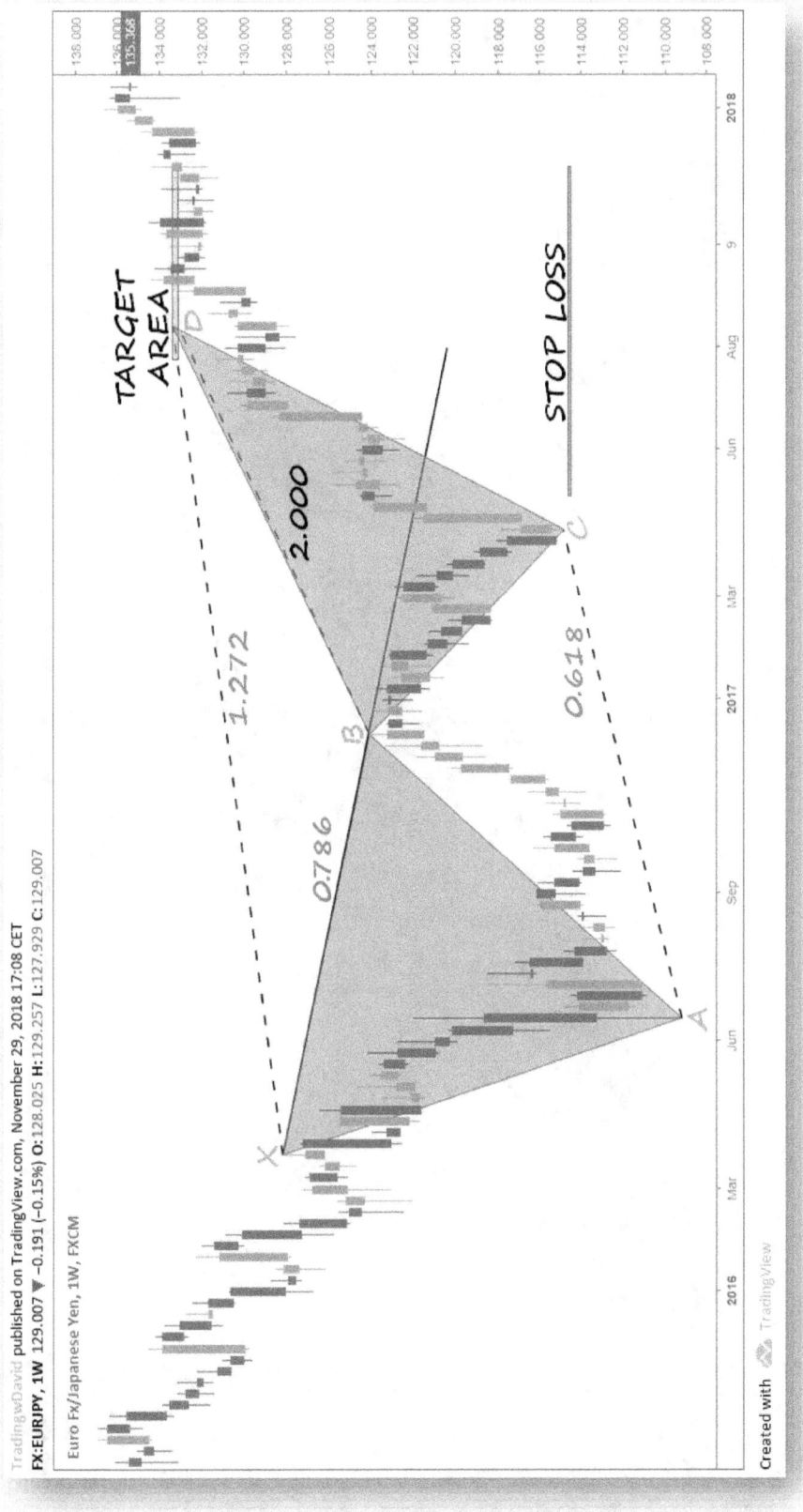

Figure 35 - Eur-Jpy, Bearish Butterfly (TradingView.com)

A Bearish Bat on Eur-Gbp weekly chart in figure 36.

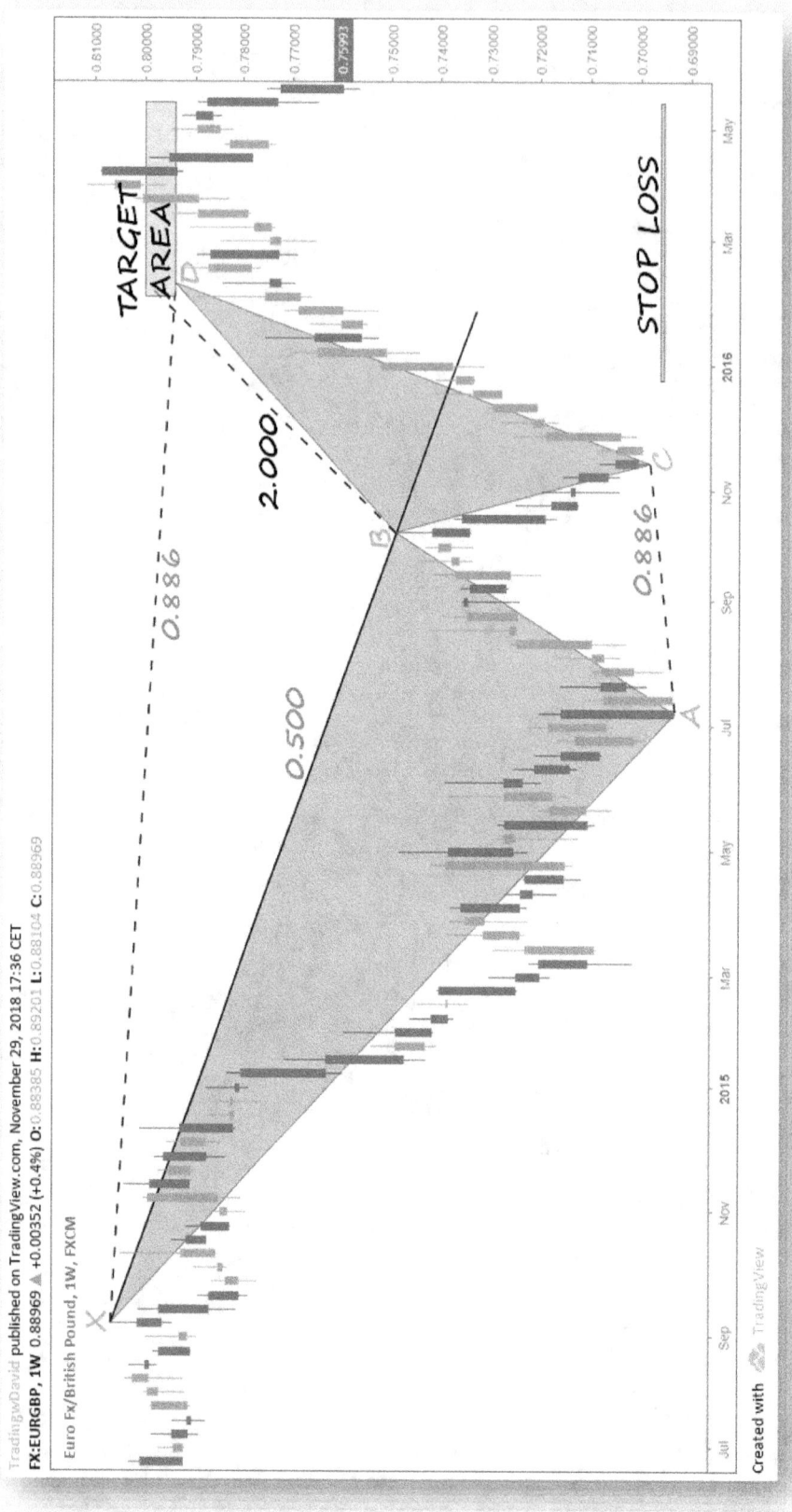

Figure 36 - Eur-Gbp, Bearish Bat (TradingView.com)

Lastly, a Bearish Crab on WTI Crude Oil daily chart in figure 37.

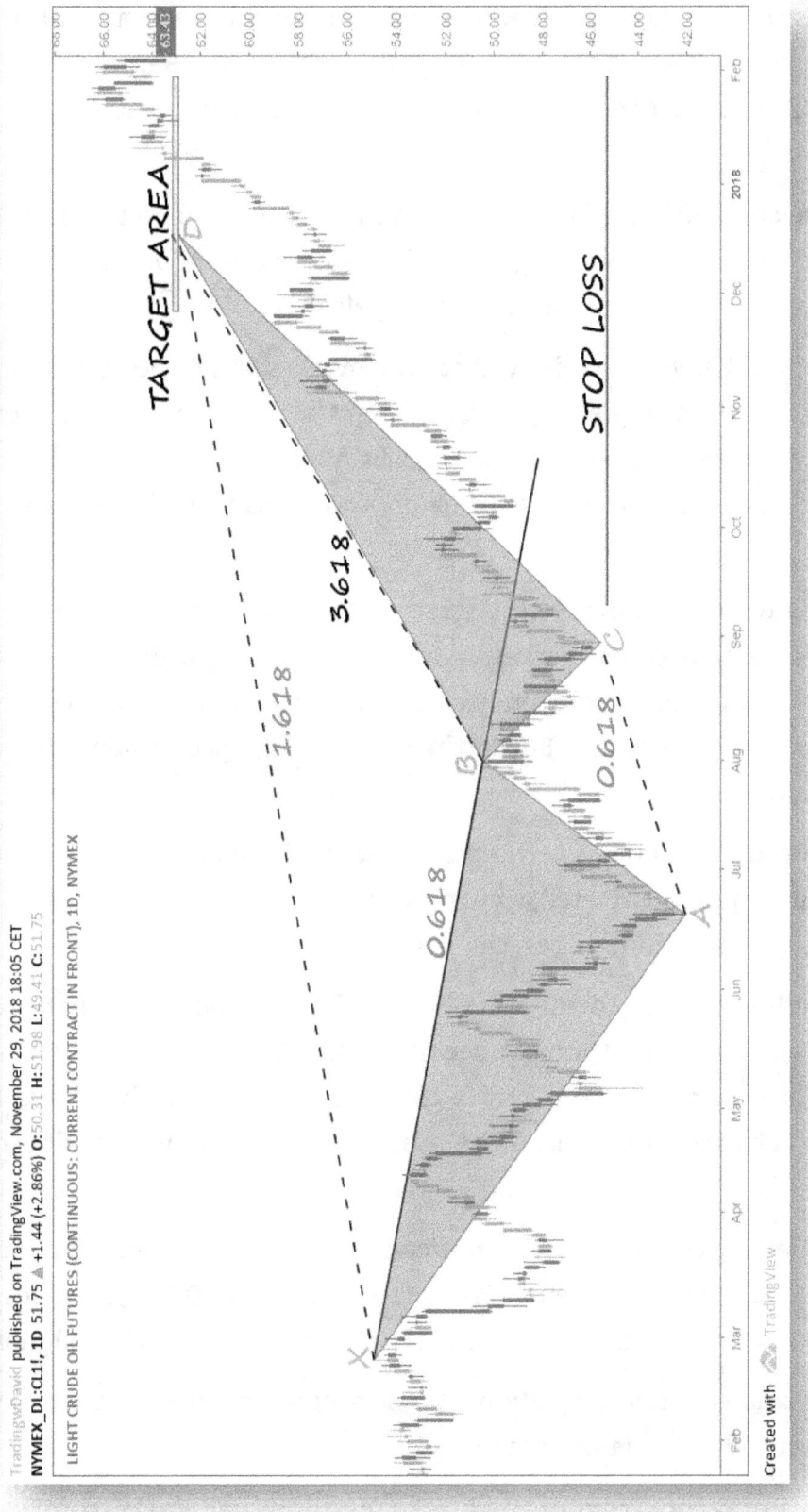

Figure 37 - WTI Crude Oil, Bearish Crab (TradingView.com)

I will not hide the fact that I felt a great satisfaction in having ridden the long rise of WTI Crude Oil. Well, I could go on for another hundred pages with examples, but I think, at this point, that this strategy is clear. Now it is just a matter of practicing, of training the eye to see possible Harmonic Patterns that are forming on the chart. Remember to apply both the correct strategy but also a correct use of money management, starting with an appropriate Position Size.

Before concluding this chapter, I want to show you some features that I figured out over time. First of all, it is a purely graphical strategy; the movement of price on a chart is the only aspect it takes into consideration, nothing else.

You should have a broader view of the market; what the macroeconomic situation is, as well as news and anything else that could significantly affect price movements. And if these do not agree with the strategy, it is always best not to risk it. Equally, you should avoid opening a trade before an important event, such as a central bank meeting or the release of earnings.

As I said, you can apply this strategy to every market. Nevertheless, it is much better suited to Forex than to other markets. A currency pair is nothing more than two opposing economies. In the medium-term, a currency pair will always tend to have a price that will reflect the real value of the two economies. But in the short-term, speculation will bring the price to move away from that level.

If there are no changes at the "fundamental" level (such as a cut in interest rates, a sharp increase in unemployment, etc.), a currency pair will move within large congestion, and more or less in a central position, that is, the "right price."

This allows for the formation of a lot of Harmonic patterns throughout the year. The stock market is different, and you can see this with most of the S&P500 equities. In the last nine years, there has been a big rise and a few short rebounds that have not allowed the formation of many Harmonic patterns. Although, occasionally, it was possible to execute a good operation.

Another aspect that I have noticed is that the retracement of BC is different between markets. Generally, it is deep in Forex (from 0.618 to 0.886), and less so in the stock market (from 0.382 to 0.618). You can use this characteristic to optimise signals.

Well, this is everything about my strategy. Below is a summary of the various levels: trade entry, stop-loss and target area.

Trade entry: breakout of the black trendline that starts from X and passes from point B (the moment in which to open the position depends on your kind of trading, aggressive or conservative).

Stop-loss: about 20/25 pips or ticks beyond point C (below point C in a bullish trade, above point C in a bearish one).

Target area: the area delimitated by the XD retracement (Gartley and Bat pattern) or XA extension (Butterfly and Crab pattern), and BC extension.

In the next chapter, I will show you a particular movement that can form on a chart, using this strategy.

Pullback

CHAPTER 3

~

Pullback is similar to the retracement that you came across in chapter two. A pullback is a falling back of a market's price from its peak, in an uptrend, or a rising back from the bottom, in a downtrend. Often, pullbacks are seen as good buying or selling opportunities. You can see an example of this in figure 38 with the Gbp-Chf daily chart.

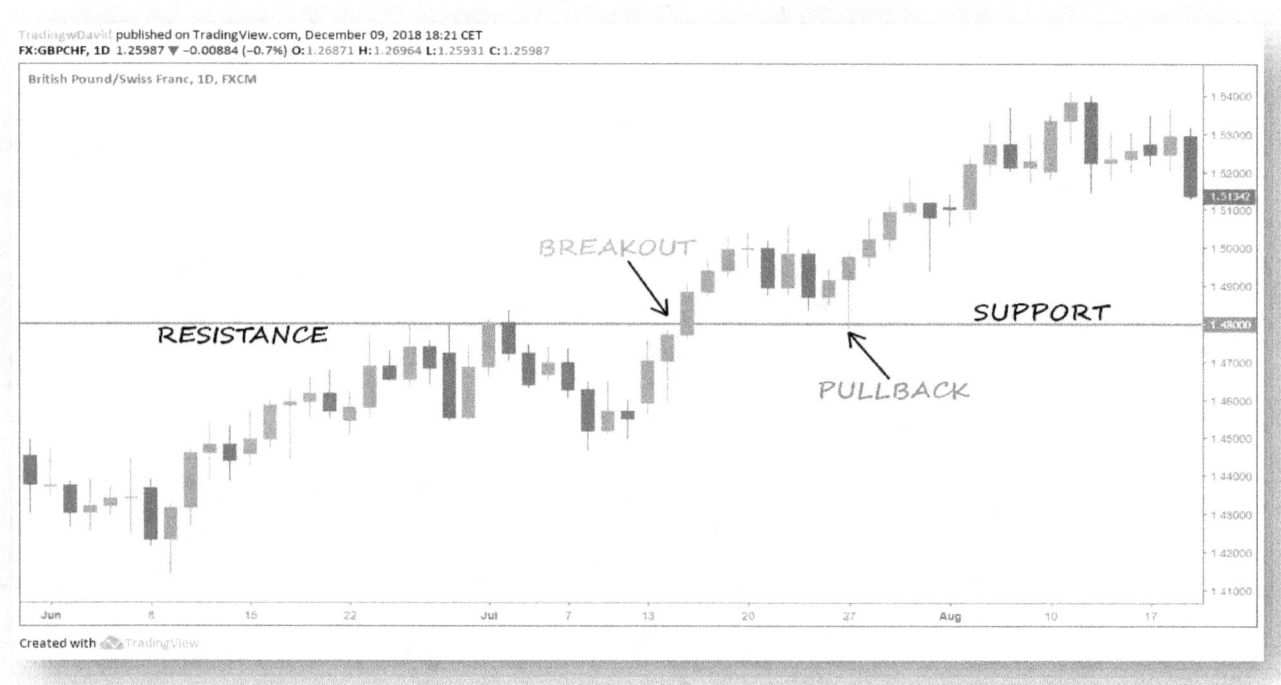

Figure 38 - Gbp-Chf, pullback (TradingView.com)

In the chart above, the price first breaks the resistance, and then it carries out a pullback retesting the old resistance (now support).

As I have said, a pullback represents a good opportunity for buying or selling an asset. This is because it confirms a breakout, therefore increasing the odds of success for the trade. This is the advantage of a pullback. The disadvantage of it is that, in waiting for a possible pullback, you risk losing good trades because a trend is too strong to carry it out.

In my strategy, pullbacks are anything but rare. I will show several examples of them on the black trendline by starting with some charts that you already came across in previous chapters.

You can see a Bullish Bat on the Eur-Usd daily chart (figure 39).

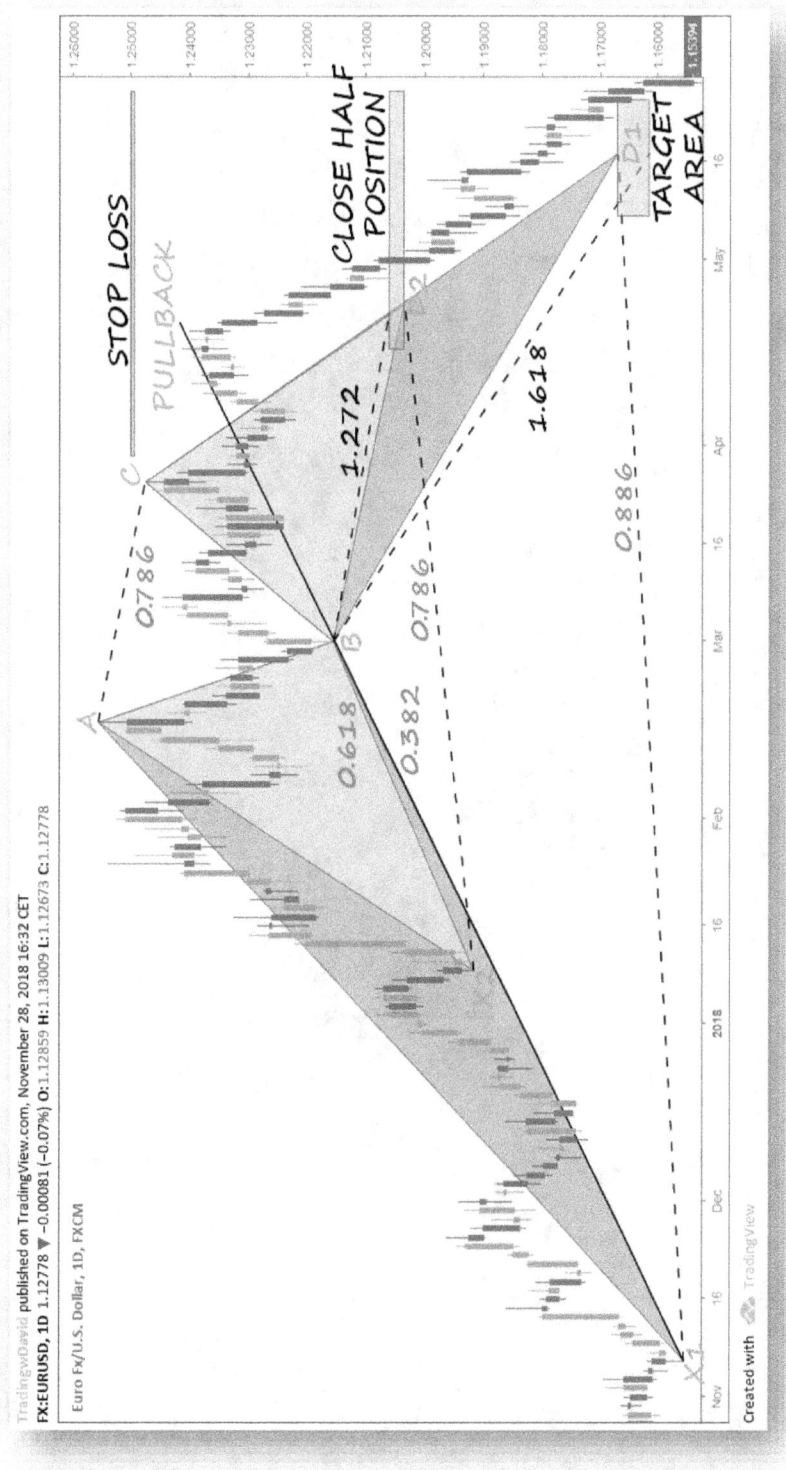

Figure 39 - Eur-Usd, Bullish Bat with pullback (TradingView.com)

A Bullish Bat on Eur-Aud daily chart in figure 40.

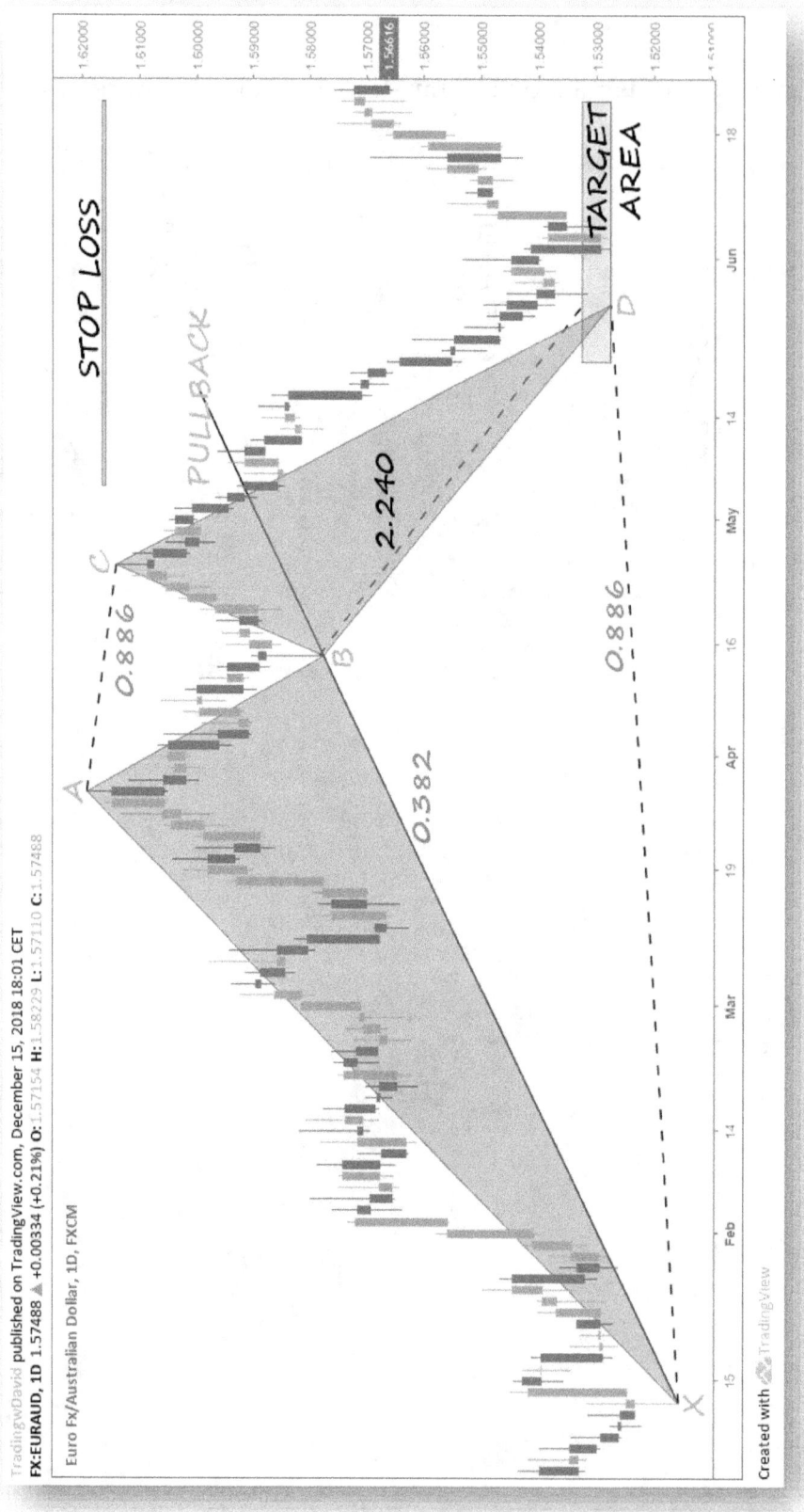

Figure 40 - Eur-Aud, Bullish Bat with pullback (TradingView.com)

A Bullish Gartley on Aud-Usd daily chart in figure 41.

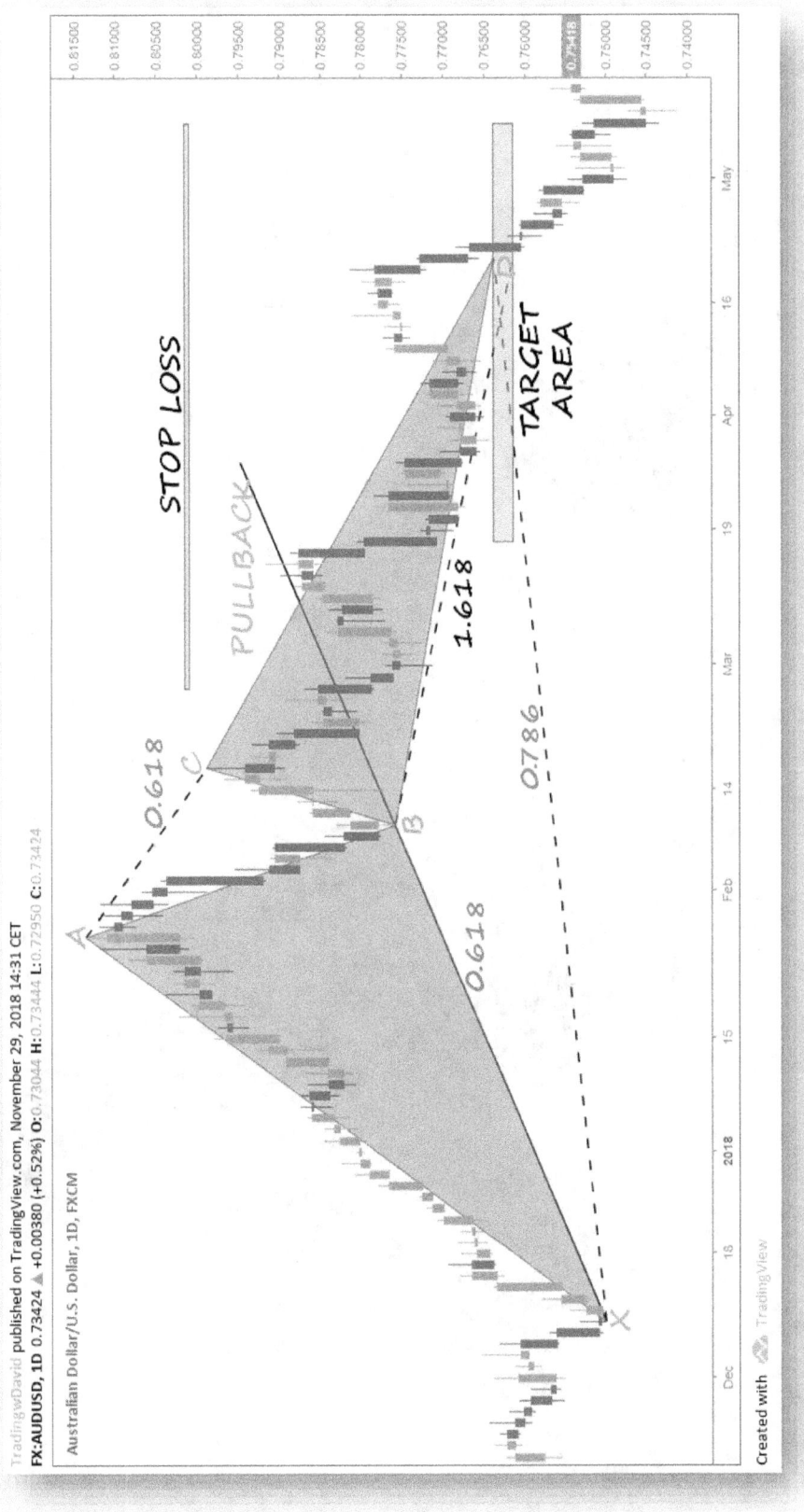

Figure 41 - Aud-Usd, Bullish Gartley with pullback (TradingView.com)

A Bearish Butterfly on Gold daily chart in figure 42.

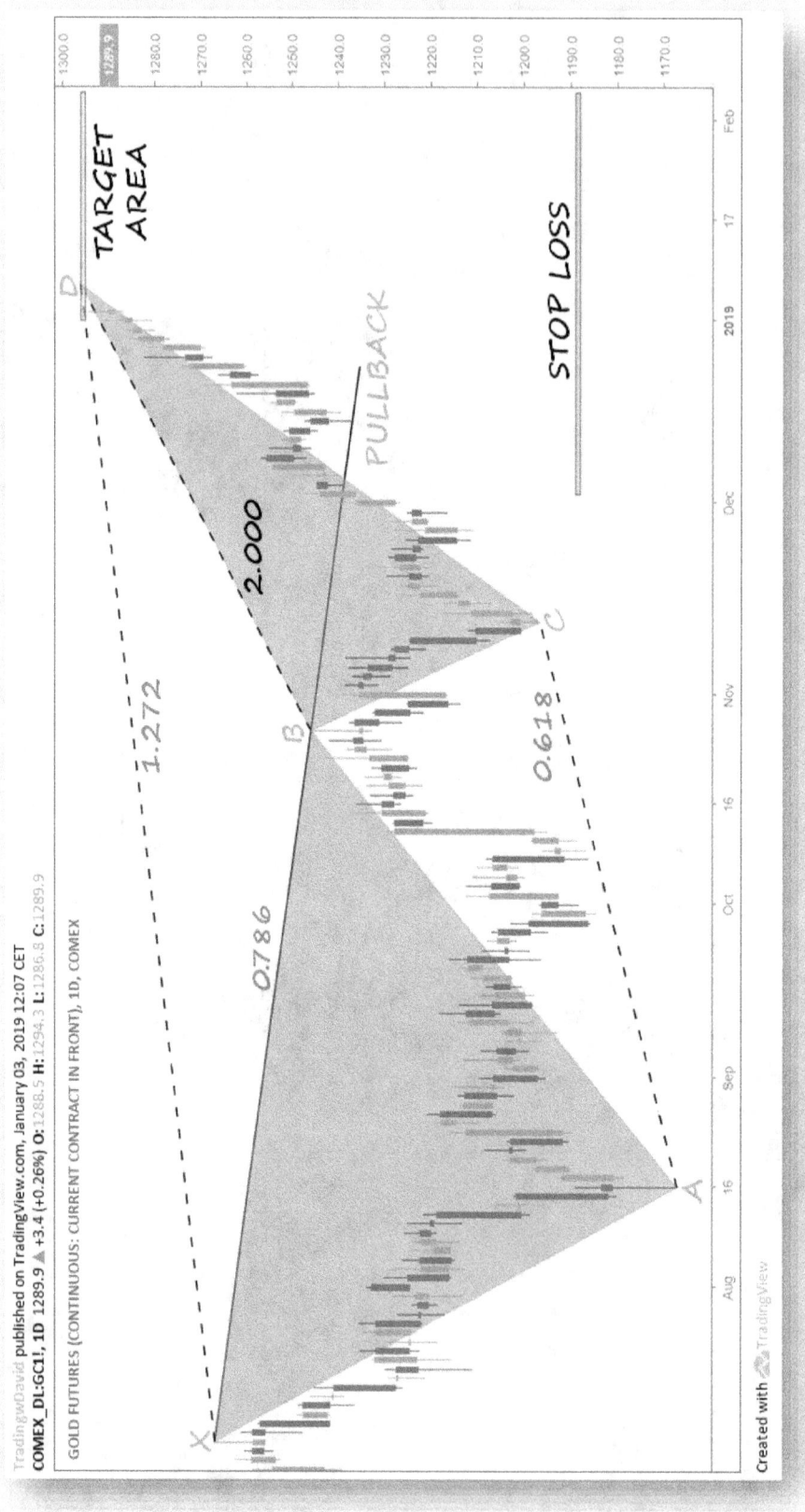

Figure 42 - Gold, Bearish Butterfly with pullback (TradingView.com)

A Bullish Bat on Eur-Chf daily chart in figure 43.

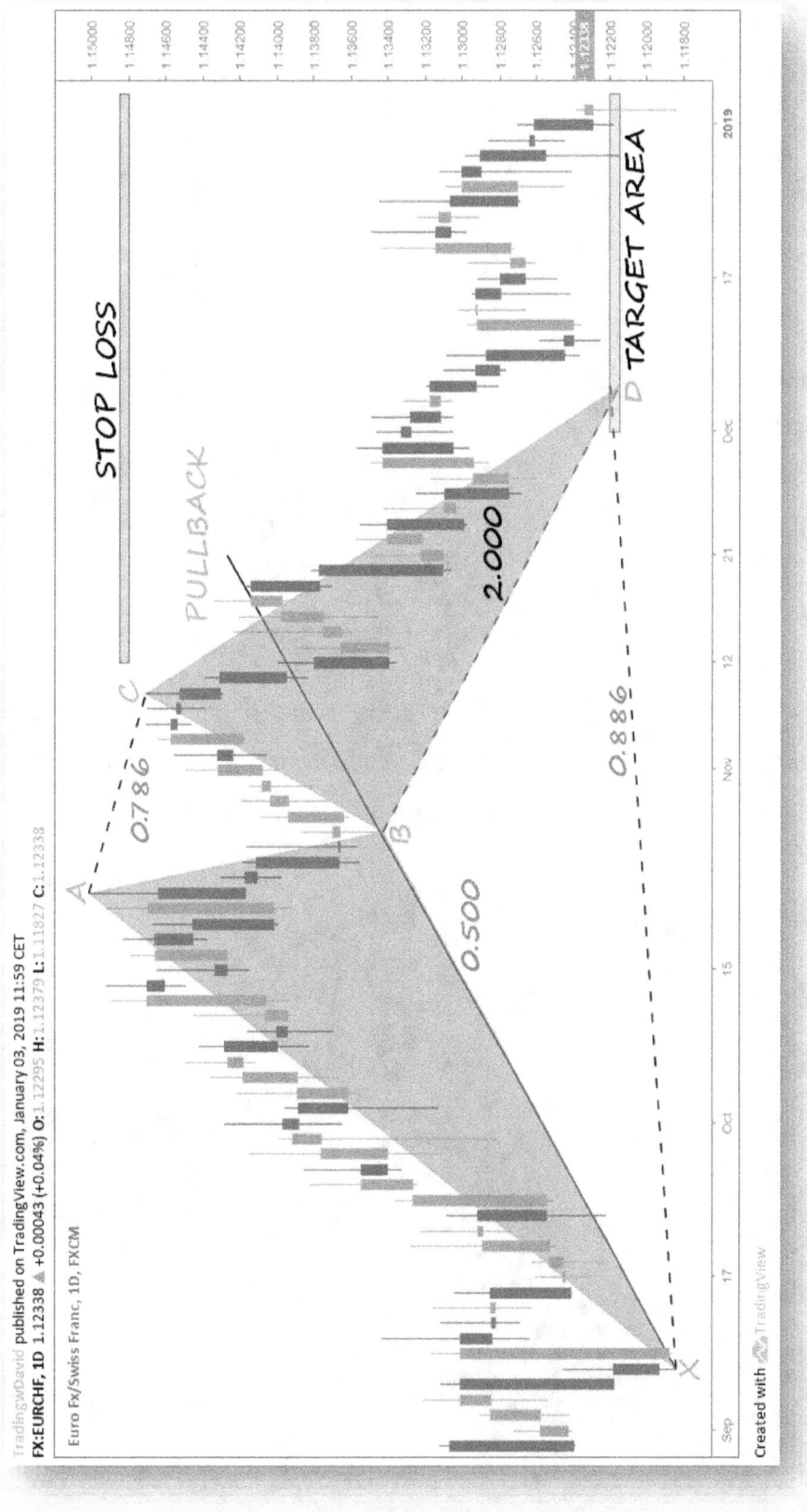

Figure 43 - Eur-Chf, Bullish Bat with pullback (TradingView.com)

A Bullish Butterfly on Google daily chart in figure 44.

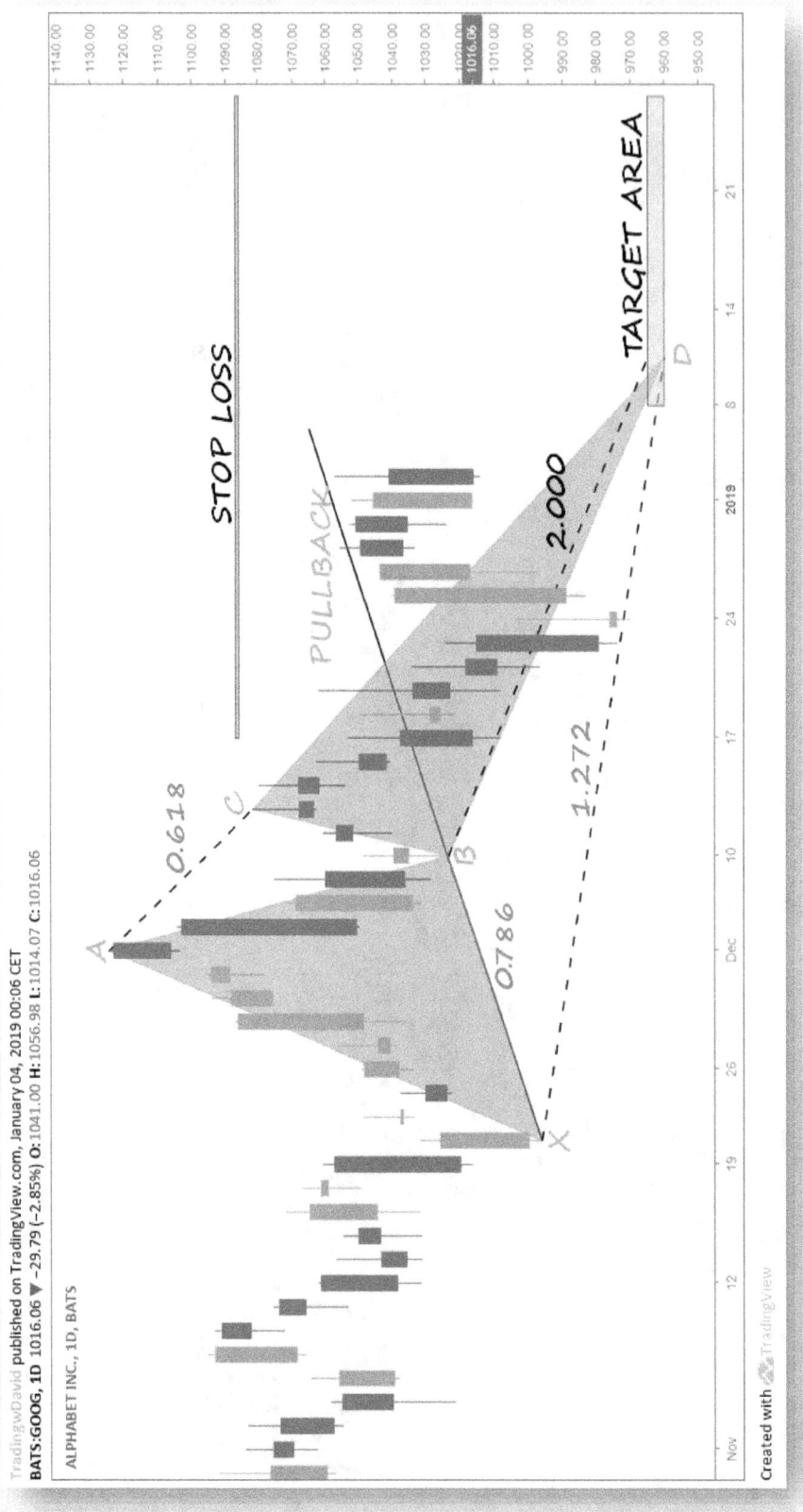

Figure 44 - Google, Bullish Butterfly with pullback (TradingView.com)

A Bullish Butterfly on Sugar daily chart in figure 45.

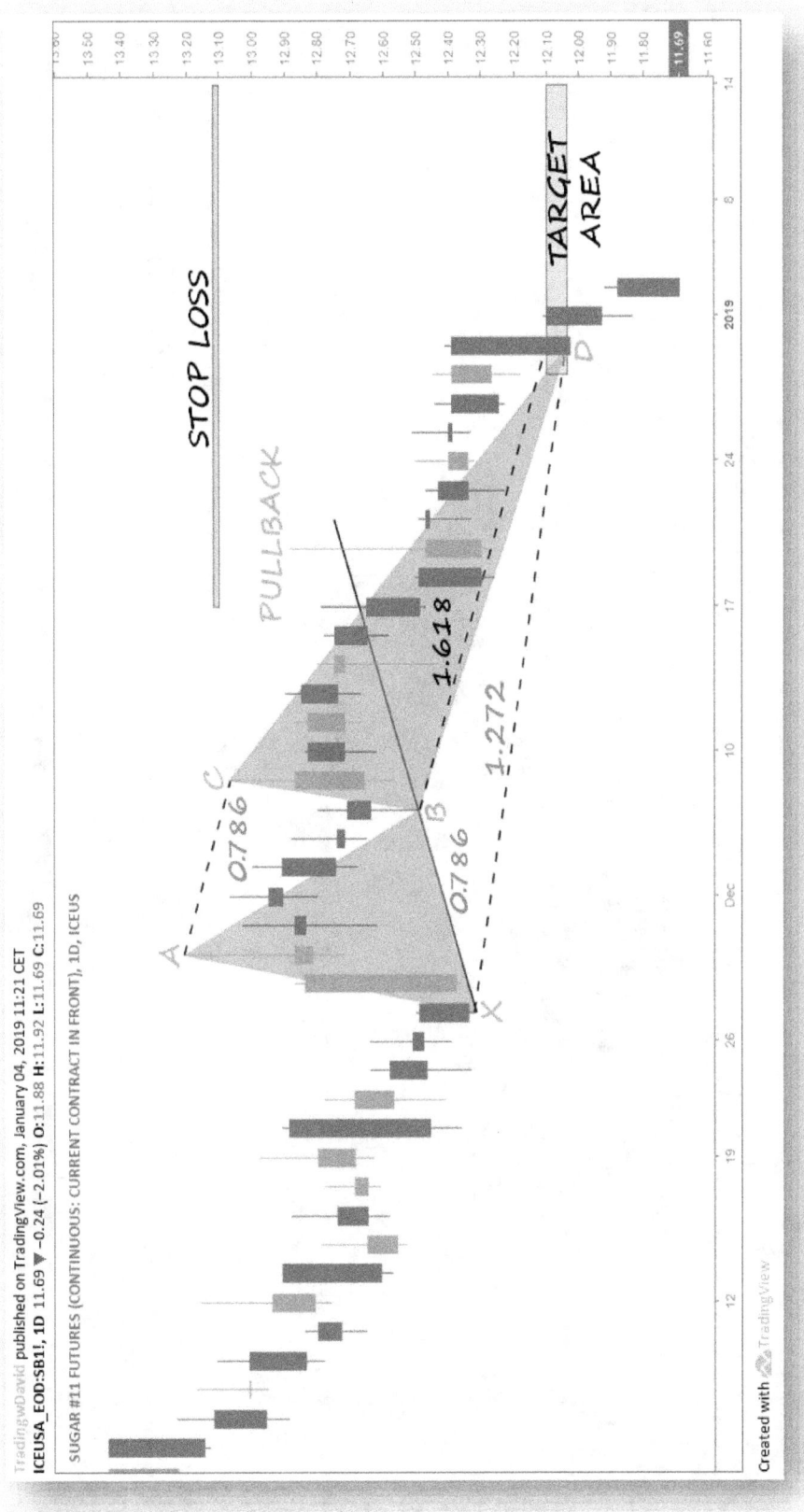

Figure 45 - Sugar, Bullish Butterfly with pullback (TradingView.com)

A Bullish Crab on Gbp-Usd daily chart in figure 46.

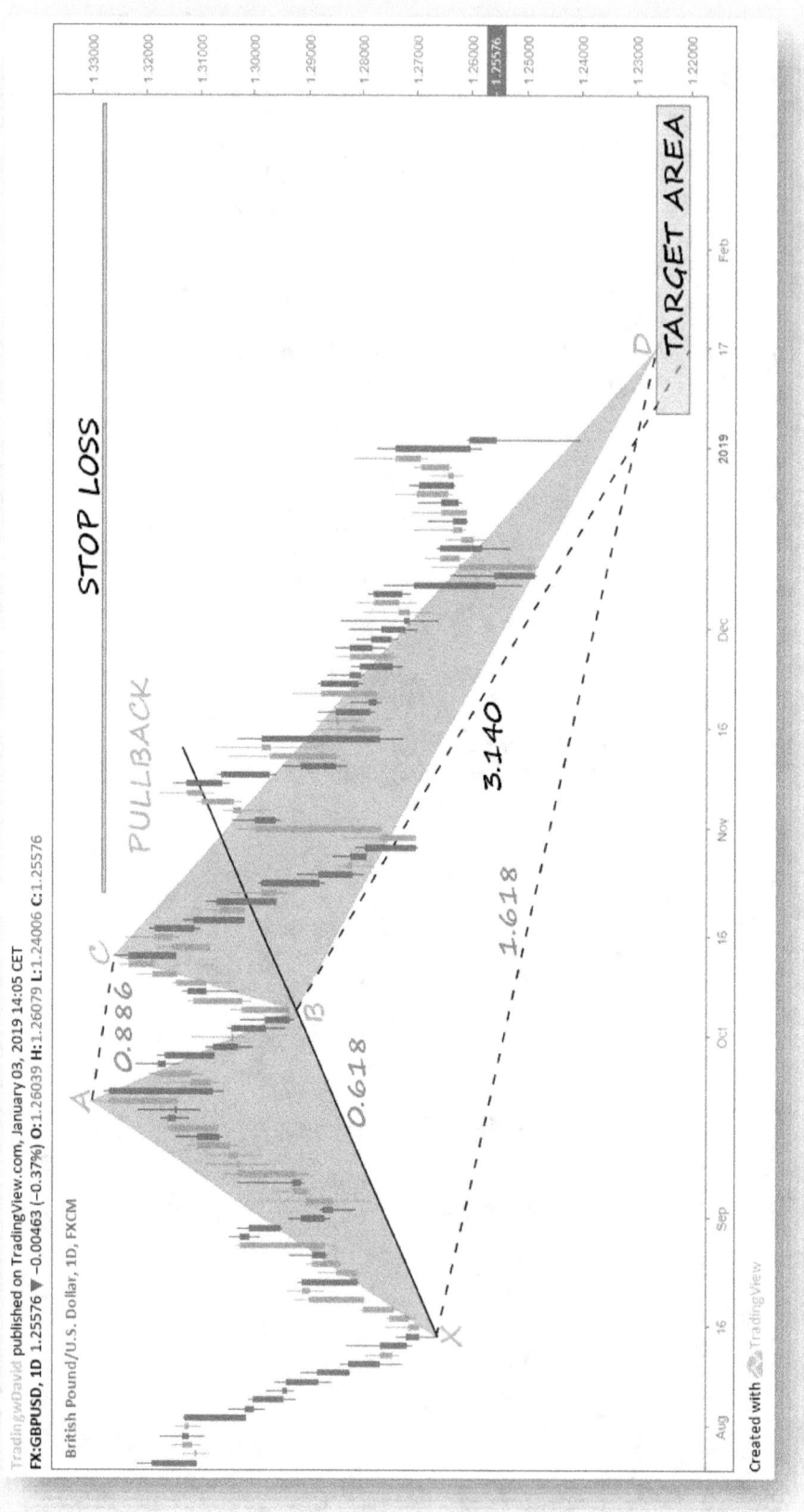

Figure 46 - Gbp-Usd, Bullish Crab with pullback (TradingView.com)

A Bearish Bat on Aud-Nzd weekly chart in figure 47.

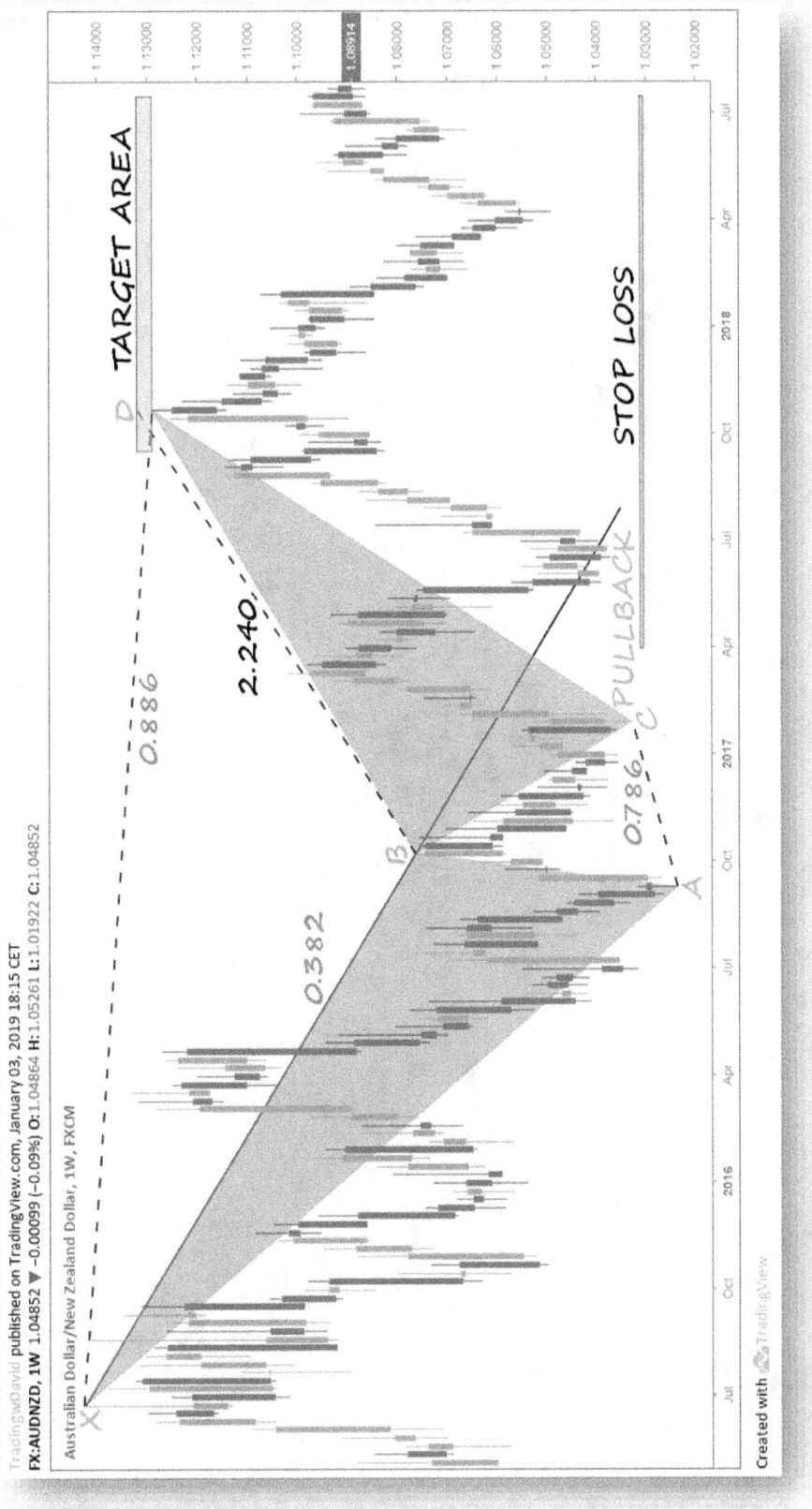

Figure 47 - Aud-Nzd, Bearish Bat with pullback (TradingView.com)

Sometimes, you may happen to see a pullback-fakeout with a price that first closes below (bullish signal) or above (bearish signal) the black trendline, and then, the next day, makes the opposite movement, cancelling the negative signal from the previous session.

You can see an example in figure 48, with the Natural Gas daily chart.

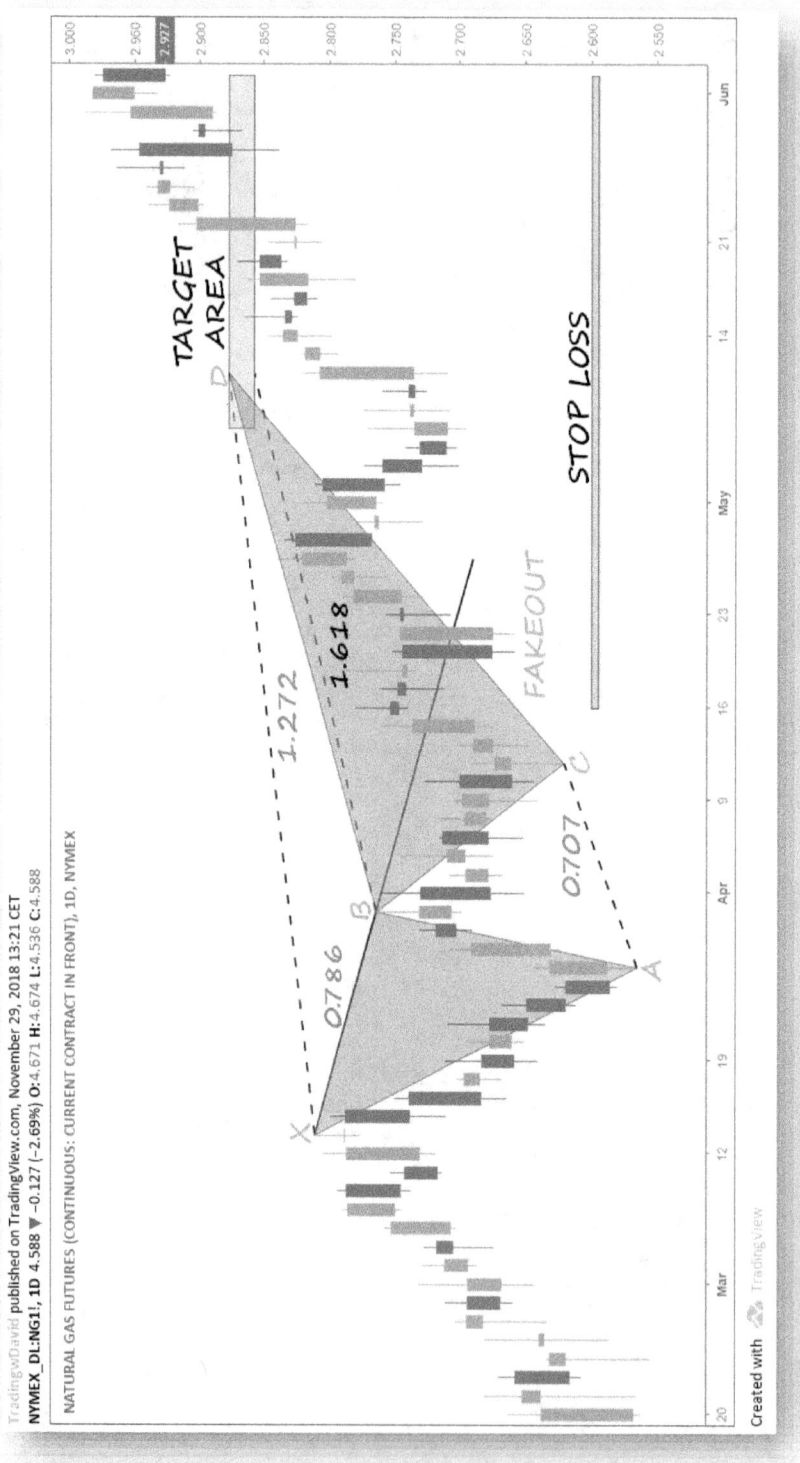

Figure 48 - Natural Gas, pullback-fakeout (TradingView.com)

In this case, after the breakout of the black trendline, and a subsequent pullback, when it seems that the price starts to rise again, a long red candle forms on the chart, with the close below the black trendline. However, in the next session, a long green candle leads the price above the black trendline again (a perfect fakeout).

You can see another example below where, similar to what happened with Natural Gas takes place in the Eur-Chad chart (figure 49).

Figure 49 - Eur-Cad, pullback-fakeout (TradingView.com)

For those who are familiar with the candlestick analysis, what has been completed straddling the black trendline above is a piercing line.

It is not very common to see this graphic formation does not happen very often, but I can tell you that in my life as a trader, every time I saw a pullback-fakeout like those above, I almost always closed my trades in profit.

In the next chapter I will offer some advice on money management by explaining how to open a position correctly.

MONEY MANAGEMENT

CHAPTER 4

It would be impossible to talk about money management in its entirety in just a couple of pages, so in this chapter I will be discussing position size in particular. In simple terms, it concerns what the correct position to open a trade is, based on the stop-loss you have decided and the maximum loss you are willing to suffer if the price reaches it.

As I specified at the beginning of the book, this strategy can be used in all the financial markets. There are different ways to calculate the position size, depending on the type of market. Below, I am going to go over the calculations for Shares, CFDs, and ETFs, and then, the one for Forex.

Stocks, CFDs, ETFs

Regardless of whether you operate with Stocks, CDFs or ETFs, the calculation is simple and always the same. Below is the formula:

Number of shares (LONG) = Max loss / (entry price – stop-loss)

Number of shares (SHORT) = Max loss / (stop-loss – entry price)

So, if for example you open a long position on Twitter with an entry price of $31.00, a stop-loss set at $28.00, and a maximum loss of $400, the number of shares to buy would be:

Number of shares (LONG) = Max loss / (entry price – stop-loss)

So:

Number of shares = $ 400 / ($ 31.00 – $ 28.00) = 133.34

According to your maximum loss and stop-loss, the number of shares you have to buy is 133. If the price reaches the stop-loss, you will lose $ 400.

If instead you establish the maximum loss not with a fixed amount of dollars (or in other currency) but with a percentage, the formula varies as follows:

Nr. of shares (LONG) = (capital x %of max loss) / (entry price – stop-loss)

Nr. of shares (SHORT) = (capital x %of max loss) / (stop-loss – entry price)

Where **capital** is the amount of money in your trading account and **%of max loss** is the maximum percentage of the money (in your account) you are willing to lose in the trade.

If for example you have an account of $ 60,000 and you decide to open a short position in Apple with entry price of $ 240.00 and stop-loss set at $ 245.00, with a maximum loss of 0.5% of the money in your account, the number of shares to sell is:

Nr. of shares (SHORT) = (capital x %of max loss) / (stop-loss – entry price)

So:

Number of shares = ($ 60,000 * 0.5%) / ($ 245.00 – $ 240.00) = 60

According to your percentage of maximum loss and your stop-loss, the number of shares you have to sell is 60. In this way, if the price hits the stop-loss, your loss will be exactly the amount you have established, $ 300 (which correspond to 0.5% of $ 60,000).

Let us now take a look at the formula for calculating the position size in Forex.

Forex

Now, I am going to show how to open a proper position in Forex according to your risk appetite. Doing this means that, even though the currency pair may reach the stop-loss, this will not create any problems for your account or cause you to stress unnecessarily.

Say, for instance, that after analysing the Gbp-Jpy daily chart, you decide to sell the currency pair with an entry level at 142.000, a stop-loss set at 143.500, and a target at 139.000. If your maximum bearable loss is $300, how much should you invest in this trade? You can obtain the position size to open this formula as follows:

Position Size = [(1,000 * max loss) / pips of stop] / value 1 pip

Where: **max loss** is your maximum bearable loss ($ 300); **pips of stop** is the distance in pips from the entry price to the stop-loss (150 in this example); the **value of 1 pip** is the minimum value of a pip for $ 1,000 of purchase/sale of the currency pair (in the example Gbp-Jpy).

For calculating the value of 1 pip of a currency pair, you can use the tool available on the Myfxbook website (https://www.myfxbook.com/forex-calculators/pip-calculator), where you simply have to select the currency in "Account Currency", 1,000 in "Trade Size" and followed by a click on "Calculate." In this way, in the table below, you will get the last column that will show you the minimum value of the pip to be used for each currency pair.

Returning to the example, the position size to open is as follows:

Position Size = [(1,000 * max loss) / pips of stop] / value 1 pip

So:

Position Size = [(1,000 * $ 300) / 150] / 0.09 = $ 22,222

The position to open is of $22,000 (rounded down, but you can also round it up if you prefer). This is a trade that, if the price hits the stop-loss, it will cause you to lose $300.

If here you establish the maximum loss (in dollars or any other currency) using a percentage rather than a fixed amount, the formula will vary, as follows:

Position Size = [(1,000 * (capital x %of max loss)) / pips of stop] / value 1 pip

And again, here **capital** means the amount of money in your trading account, and **%of max loss** refers to the maximum percentage of money in your account that you are willing to lose in the trade.

If for example you have an account of $ 50,000 and you decide to open a long position on Eur-Chf with entry price of 1.1720, stop-loss set at 1.1580, and a maximum loss of 0.75%, the position size to open would be:

Position Size = [(1,000 * (capital x %of max loss)) / pips of stop] / value 1 pip

So:

Position Size = [(1,000 * ($ 50,000 x 0.75%)) / 140] / 0.10 = $ 26,785

The position to open is of $26,750 (rounded down). A trade that, if price hits the stop-loss, will cause a loss of $375, that is, of 0.75$ of your account.

What you have seen in this chapter is only a part of your money management and trading plan. Remember that you always have to put yourself in the best conditions to trade.

Final Comments

CHAPTER 5

What you have seen in this book is my personal way of using Harmonic Patterns. Do not be deceived into underestimating this book because I distribute it for free. If you use this strategy correctly, and with the appropriate money management, it will yield very high percentages of trades closed in gain.

This strategy works on all the time-frames, Although the greater the time-frame, the more accurate the signals will be. I apply it, apart from a few rare exceptions, on daily charts. I have not written anything about managing positions. It is an argument that is not easy to deal with and is undoubtedly the most essential and challenging part of a trade. However, I do want to impart a couple of tips, dictated by my twenty-five years of experience in trading.

As you have seen from the examples, this strategy almost always has an excellent R/R (Risk/Reward). This aspect allows you to do two things.

The first is to move the stop-loss at break-even when the price has earned the same number of pips or ticks as your stop. I will explain to you better with an example. You open a long position on a currency pair with a stop-loss of 150 pips.

When your trade gets a profit of 150 pips, you can move the stop-loss at break-even (at the same level as your trade entry). In this way, you will no longer risk anything; it will be a trade risk-free. Believe me that there is nothing more mortifying in trading than seeing a profitable trade closed at a loss. You must avoid this happening.

The second thing you can do is close a part of the position (in gain) once you reach a specified level. You can decide to close part of the position when the price reaches, for example, a static support/resistance, or when your profit is 50% (or another percentage) of the target; it is up to you and your trading. And if you also move the stop at break-even, you will be sure to make a profit.

As I said, this strategy generates a good percentage of trades closed in gain. But no strategy is perfect. I want to show you a trade that I did with the options on Natural Gas. In figure 50 is the daily chart.

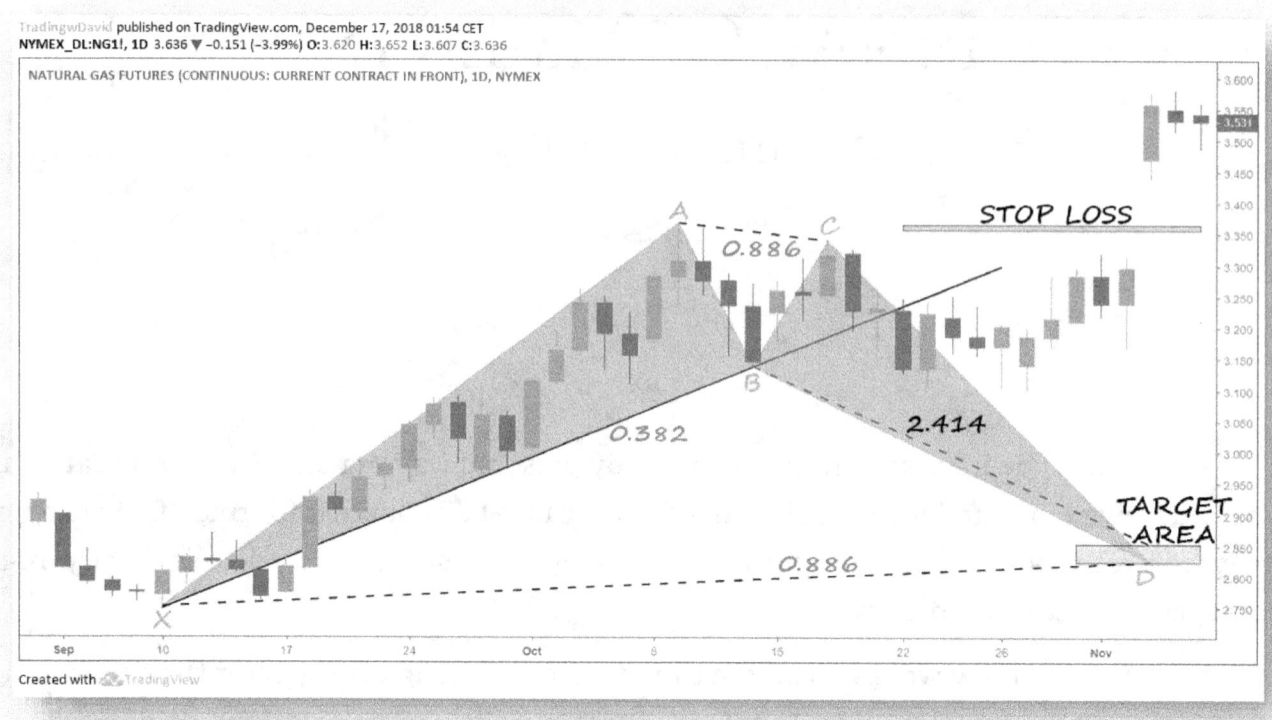

Figure 50 – Natural Gas daily chart (TradingView.com)

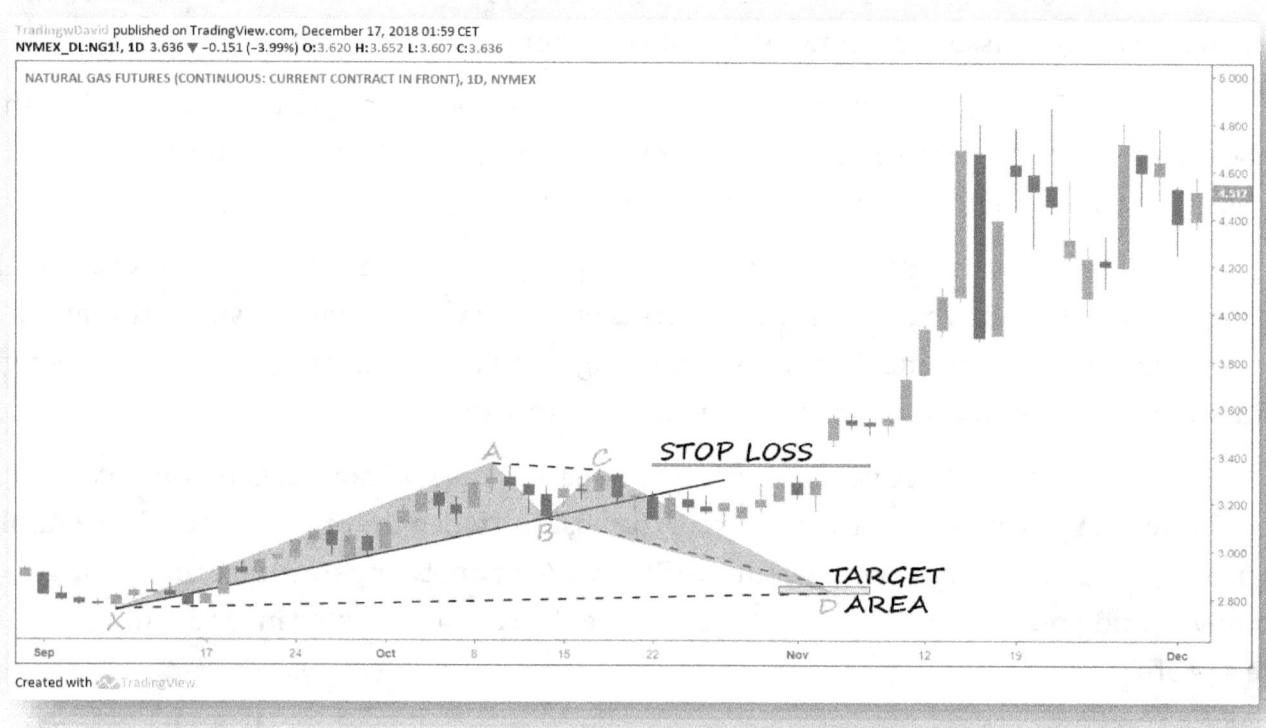

Figure 51 – Natural Gas daily chart (TradingView.com)

On Sunday, the price opened in gap up, above the stop-loss. So, I had to close my trade at a loss, and at an even worse price than I had decided in my analysis. But look at what happened over the next few days. As you can see in figure 51 above, a few days later, the price exploded upwards. In four days, +40%.

This example aims to encourage you to always respect all the rules you have seen explained. The strategy is profitable only if you are disciplined in applying it. And furthermore, it gives me the opportunity, at the end of this book, to repeat a concept which I consider very important.

What I have explained to you is a purely graphical strategy. It does not consider anything else. It would be wise to take a look at macro data, news, fundamentals and anything that can significantly influence the price. If there are mixed signals, it is always better to let go of a trade. However, concerning the natural gas example, there was actually nothing to suggest such a strong rise.

This book has come to an end. This strategy gives me a lot of satisfaction, and I am sure that, if you use it correctly, it will be the same for you. I conclude by thanking from the bottom of my heart Caroline for her efforts in proofreading this book into English, she was very kind and professional. You can contact her through her email: carolinewinter4@hotmail.com.

For any questions my email is info@tradingwithdavid.com. On my website https://tradingwithdavid.com you can find articles, analysis, books, and much more. You find my other books on Amazon: **https://amazon.com/author/davidcarli**.

You can also follow me on:

- **Twitter**: https://twitter.com/tradingwdavid;
- **Instagram**: https://www.instagram.com/tradingwithdavidoriginal/, with operational ideas and discussions of economics and financial markets;
- **YouTube**: https://www.youtube.com/channel/UCHB18Qsl0fm-eBULQEMsVSA;
- **TradingView**: https://www.tradingview.com/u/TradingwDavid.

Do not go yet; one last thing to do.

If you enjoyed this book or found it useful, I would be very grateful if you would post a short review on Amazon. Your support does make a difference, and I read all the reviews personally so I can get your feedback and make this book even better.

Thanks in advance for your support! I really hope that what you have read will help you in your trading.

Happy Trading to you all!

STRATEGY PARAMETERS

APPENDIX A

SUMMARY TABLE WITH HARMONIC PATTERNS AND PARAMETERS

PATTERN	POINT B	POINT C	D (TARGET)
GARTLEY	0.618XA	0.382AB	0.786XA
	0.618XA	0.500AB	0.786XA
	0.618XA	0.618AB	0.786XA
	0.618XA	0.707AB	0.786XA
	0.618XA	0.786AB	0.786XA
	0.618XA	0.886AB	0.786XA
BAT	0.328XA	0.382AB	0.886XA
	0.328XA	0.500AB	0.886XA
	0.328XA	0.618AB	0.886XA
	0.328XA	0.707AB	0.886XA
	0.328XA	0.786AB	0.886XA
	0.328XA	0.886AB	0.886XA
	0.500XA	0.382AB	0.886XA

BUTTERFLY	0.500XA	0.500AB	0.886XA
	0.500XA	0.618AB	0.886XA
	0.500XA	0.707AB	0.886XA
	0.500XA	0.786AB	0.886XA
	0.500XA	0.886AB	0.886XA
	0.786XA	0.382AB	1.272XA
	0.786XA	0.500AB	1.272XA
	0.786XA	0.618AB	1.272XA
	0.786XA	0.707AB	1.272XA
	0.786XA	0.786AB	1.272XA
	0.786XA	0.886AB	1.272XA
CRAB	0.382XA	0.382AB	1.618XA
	0.382XA	0.500AB	1.618XA
	0.382XA	0.618AB	1.618XA
	0.382XA	0.707AB	1.618XA
	0.382XA	0.786AB	1.618XA
	0.382XA	0.886AB	1.618XA
	0.500XA	0.382AB	1.618XA
	0.500XA	0.500AB	1.618XA
	0.500XA	0.618AB	1.618XA
	0.500XA	0.707AB	1.618XA
	0.500XA	0.786AB	1.618XA

0.500XA	0.886AB	1.618XA
0.618XA	0.382AB	1.618XA
0.618XA	0.500AB	1.618XA
0.618XA	0.618AB	1.618XA
0.618XA	0.707AB	1.618XA
0.618XA	0.786AB	1.618XA
0.618XA	0.886AB	1.618XA

Table 1 - Summary harmonic patterns with all parameters

WEB RESOURCES

APPENDIX B

Below, summarised, are all the resources you have seen in this book, as well as others.

WEBSITE	LINK
Free Platform	
TradingView	https://www.tradingview.com
Follow me	
Website	https://tradingwithdavid.com
Twitter	https://twitter.com/tradingwdavid
Instagram	https://www.instagram.com/tradingwithdavidoriginal
YouTube	https://www.youtube.com/channel/UCHB18Qsl0fm-eBULQEMsVSA
TradingView	https://www.tradingview.com/u/TradingwDavid
Tools	
Pip Calculator	https://www.myfxbook.com/forex-calculators/pip-calculator
Resources	
Economic Calendar	https://tradingwithdavid.com/economic-calendar

Table 2 - Web resources

www.ingramcontent.com/pod-product-compliance
Lightning Source LLC
Chambersburg PA
CBHW080525220526
45465CB00006B/2600